CREATION *and*
the TIMELESS
ORDER
of THINGS

CREATION and the TIMELESS ORDER of THINGS

ESSAYS IN ISLAMIC
MYSTICAL PHILOSOPHY

BY TOSHIHIKO IZUTSU

WITH A FOREWORD BY WILLIAM C. CHITTICK

WHITE CLOUD PRESS
ASHLAND, OREGON

99 98 97 96 95   5 4 3 2 1

Cover Design by Dan Cook
Printed in the United States of America

LIBRARY OF CONGRESS CATALOGING IN PUBLICATION DATA

Izutsu, Toshihiko, 1914-1993
    Creation and the timeless order of things: essays in Islamic mystical philosophy / by Toshihiko Izutsu
        p.   cm.
    Includes bibliographical references.
    ISBN 1-883991-04-8 : $16.00
    1. Sufism--Iran--History. 2. Sufism--Doctrines--History.
    I. Title.
    BP188.8.I55I98   1994
    297'.4--dc20   93-48946
                                                            CIP

CONTENTS

The Basic Structure of Metaphysical Thinking in Islam   *1*

The Paradox of Light and Darkness in the
     Garden Mysteries off Shabastarí   *38*

An an analysis of *wahdat al-wujúd*   *66*

Mysticism and the Linguistic Problem of Equivocation
     in the Thought of 'Ayn al-Qudat al-Hamadáni   *98*

Creation and the Timeless Order of Things: A Study in the
     Mystical Philosophy of 'Ayn al-Qudat al-Hamadáni   *119*

The Concept of Perpetual Creation in Islamic Mysticism
     and Zen Buddhism   *141*

Existentialism East and West   *174*

Index of Names and Technical Terms   *187*

The essays in this collection originally appeared in the following books and journals.

"The Basic Structure of Metaphysical Thinking in Islam." In *Collected Papers on Islamic Philosophy and Mysticism, Wisdom of Persia Series*, vol. 4, ed. M. Mohaghedh and H. Landolt, 39-72. Tehran: McGill University, 1971.

"The Paradox of Light and Darkness in the Garden Mysteries of Shabastárí." In *Anagogic Qualities of Literature*, edited by Joseph P. Strelka, 288-307. University Park, PA: Univerisity of Pennsylvania Press, 1971.

"An analysis of wahdat al-wujúd: Toward a Metaphilosophy of Oriental Philosophies." In *The Concept and Reality of Existence* by Toshihiko Izutsu, 35-55. Tokyo: Keio Instute of Cultural and Linguistic Studies, 1971.

"Mysticism and the Linguistic Problem of Equivocation in the Thought of 'Ayn al-Qudat al-Hamadání," *Studia Islamica* 30 (1970): 153-70.

"Creation and the Timeless Order of Things: A Study in the Mystical Philosophy of 'Ayn al-Qudat al-Hamadání," *Philosophical Forum* 4:1 (1972): 124-40.

"The Concept of Perpetual Creation in the Islamic Mysticism and Zen Buddhism." In *Melange offerts à Henry Corbin*, ed. S.H. Nasr, 115-48. Tehran: Iranian Academy of Philosophy, 1977.

"Existentialism East and West," In *The Concept and Reality of Existence* by Toshihiko Izutsu, 25-33. Tokyo: Keio Instute of Cultural and Linguistic Studies, 1971.

FOREWORD

I FIRST MET PROFESSOR IZUTSU in 1971 when he and Professor
Hermann Landolt came to Tehran to do research at the Tehran
branch of the McGill Institute of Islamic Studies, which had
been established under the guidance of Professor Medhi Mo-
haghegh in 1969. By that time, I have finished my course work
in the Persian language and its literature at Tehran University
and had begun work on my Ph.D. dissertation, a critical edition of 'Abd al-Rahmán Jámí's *Naqd al-nusús fí sharh naqsh al-
fusús.* When Professor Izutsu made arrangements to spend three
months a year in Tehran doing research, three of us—myself
plus Gholamreza Aavani and Nasrollah Pourjavady, both of
whom are now well known scholars in Iran—asked him to
read Ibn al-'Arabí's *Fusús al-hikam* with us. We began meeting
once a week on April 21, 1972. At each meeting we would
laboriously read short passages from the text and then translate
them into English, and Professor Izutsu would correct our read-
ings and situate passages in the context of Ibn al-'Arabí's
thought. In the fall of 1974, Professor Izutsu left McGill University and joined the Imperial Academy of Philosophy, which

had just been founded under the directorship of Seyyed Hossein Nasr. We continued reading the *Fusús* as an official class at the Academy until we finished the text in March, 1978, being joined at one time or another over the years by several other students.

Professor Izutsu had an extraordinary grasp of the intricacies of the Arabic language. The *Fusús* is one of the most difficult texts in Islamic thought, not only because of the inherent difficulty of the ideas, but also because of grammatical and linguistic issues that arise in many obscure passages. Izutsu had read the important commentaries carefully, and he would usually present us with the alternative interpretations that had been proposed. Then he would explain the reasons for his own preference, which did not always agree with any of the commentators. His remarks were always clear, precise, and carefully weighed. More than anything, Izutsu's students owe to him an awareness of the importance of careful analysis of the grammatical and linguistic structure of philosophical and Sufi texts.

Once we asked Professor Izutsu how he ended up studying Islamic texts. He replied that as a child, he had been forced by his father to perform *zazen*, and he had been intensely repelled by the experience. As a result, he decided to enter into a field that was as far away as possible from the Zen approach to reality, and hence he chose linguistics. He set out to learn several foreign languages, and by the age of eighteen he was teaching Russian at the university level. At the first opportunity that presented itself, he also learned Arabic, not to mention Persian, Turkish, and several European and Indian languages. From the study of Arabic, it was only a short distance to his careful analyses of the Koran's linguistic structure, such as *God and Man in the Koran: Semantics of the Koranic Weltanschuung.*

Fortunately for all of us, Professor Izutsu's antipathy for Zen quickly disappeared, as works such as *Towards a Philosophy of Zen Buddhism* and *Celestial Journey: Far Eastern Ways of*

Thinking amply illustrate. His linguistic virtuosity, combined with penetrating insight into the underlying ideas and motivations of religious and mystical works, has given us a series of unparalleled studies of the Koran, Sufism, and Islamic philosophy. His genius at close reading comes out clearly in the essays gathered in this volume. Too many scholars have presented us with sweeping generalizations about Islamic thought rather than careful attention to the nuances of texts. Though not afraid of making broad judgments, Prof. Izutsu deserves special recognition for the clarity and sympathy with which he investigates the intricate modalities of Islamic philosophical thinking. Everyone interested in the deeper dimensions of Islamic thought owes a debt of gratitude to White Cloud Press for making these essays available in one volume.

William C. Chittick
Mt. Sinai, New York
March 1, 1994

CHAPTER 1

THE BASIC STRUCTURE OF METAPHYSICAL THINKING IN ISLAM

IN THIS OPENING ESSAY, I want to draw attention to one of the most important types of the philosophical activity within Eastern philosophy as exemplified by the thought of some of the outstanding philosophers of Iran. I believe this approach has some significance in the particular context of East-West encounter and the aim of creating and promoting a better mutual understanding between East and West at the level of philosophical thinking. It is my conviction that the realization of a true international friendship or brotherhood among the nations of the East and West, based on a deep philosophical understanding of the ideas and thoughts of each other, is one of the things that are most urgently needed in the present-day situation of the world.

Unlike Western philosophy, however, which presents a fairly conspicuous uniformity of historical development from its pre-Socratic origin down to its contemporary forms, there is in the East no such historical uniformity. We can only speak of Eastern philosophies in the plural.

Such being the case, it is, I think, very important that the various philosophies of the East be studied in a systematic way with a view to arriving at a comprehensive structural framework, a kind of meta-philosophy of the Eastern philosophies, by means of which the major Oriental philosophies may be brought up to a certain level of structural uniformity.

In other words, before we begin to think of the possibility of a fruitful philosophical understanding between East and West, we shall have to actualize a better philosophical under-standing within the confines of the Oriental philosophical traditions themselves. It is with such an idea in mind that I approach the problem of the basic structure of metaphysical thinking in Islam.

Islam has produced in the course of its long history a number of outstanding thinkers and a variety of philosophical schools. Here I shall pick up only one of them, which is known as the school of the "unity of existence" and which is un-doubtedly one of the most important. This concept, unity of existence, goes back to a great Arab mystic-philosopher of Spain of the eleventh and twelfth centuries, Ibn 'Arabí (1165-1240 C.E.). It exercised a tremendous influence upon the majority of Mus-lim thinkers, particularly in Iran, in the periods extending from the thirteenth century down to the sixteenth and seven-teenth centuries, when the tradition of Islamic metaphysical thinking found its culminating and all-synthesizing point in the thought of Sadr al-Dín Shírází, commonly known as Mullá Sadrá (1571-1640 C.E.).

Thus the scope of this essay is a very limited one, both

historically and geographically. But the problems I am going to discuss are those that belong to the most fundamental dimension of metaphysical thinking in general. Moreover, I would like to point out that the "unity of existence" school of thought is not, for Islam, a thing of the past. On the contrary, the tradition is still vigorously alive in present-day Iran. I hope that my presentation of the problems will shed some light on the position occupied by Iran in the philosophical world of the East.

As one of the most salient features of the Iranian thought *vocab* in the periods just mentioned, we may begin by pointing out an unremitting search for something eternal and absolute beyond the world of relative and transient things. Formulated in this way, it may sound a truism; in fact it is a feature com- *vocab* . monly shared by almost all religions. The important point, however, is that this problem was raised in Islam in terms of the *reality* of existence. "Existence" (*wujúd*) is here the central key term.

In order to elucidate the real significance of this idea in its historical context I must explain briefly what is usually known in the West as the thesis of the "accidentality of existence" attributed to Avicenna, or Ibn Sínā (980-1037 C.E.). This notorious thesis was attributed to Avicenna first by Averroes, or Ibn Rushd (1126-1198 C.E.), a famous Arab philosopher of Spain of the twelfth century, and then in the West by Thomas Aquinas who followed Averroes in the understanding of Avicenna's position. In the light of what we now know of Avicenna's thought, their understanding was a misinterpretation. But the Avicennian position as misinterpreted by Averroes and Thomas played a very important role not only in the East but also in the history of Western philosophy.

In fact, from the earliest phase of the historical development of Islamic philosophy, the concept of "existence" (*wujúd*), as a heritage from Greek philosophy, was the greatest metaphysical problem the Muslim thinkers had to face. The problem was first raised explicitly by al-Fárábí (872-950 C.E.), and it was presented in an extraordinary form by Avicenna when he declared that "existence" is an accident (*'arad*) of "quiddity" (*máhíyah*).

The most important question which we must ask here is: What did Avicenna really intend to convey by the above-statement? I must first clarify this point.

We constantly use in our daily conversation propositions whose subject is a noun and whose predicate is an adjective: for example: "The flower is white," "This table is brown," etc. On the same model we can easily transform an existential proposition like: "The table is" or "The table exists" into "The table is existent." Thus transformed, "existence" is just an adjective denoting a quality of the table. And the proposition "the table is existent" stands quite on a par with the proposition "the table is brown," for in both cases the subject is a noun denoting a substance called "table," while the predicate is an adjective indicating grammatically a property or accident of the substance.

It is on this level and on this level only, that Avicenna speaks of existence being an "accident" of essence. Otherwise expressed, it is at the level of logical or grammatical analysis of reality that it makes sense to maintain the accidentality of existence. However, neither Averroes nor Thomas Aquinas understood the Avicennian thesis in that way. They thought that "existence" in the thought of Avicenna must be a property inhering in a substance, not only at the level of logical or grammatical analysis of reality but in terms of the very structure of the objective, external reality. That is to say, "existence" according to Avicenna must be a predicamental or categorical accident, understood in the sense of *ens in alio*,

something existing in something else, i.e. a real property qualifying real substances, just in the same way as other ordinary
properties, like whiteness existing in a flower, coldness existing in ice, or brownness existing in a table.

It is clear that the Avicennian position, once understood
in such a way, will immediately lead to an absurd conclusion;
namely, that the table would have to exist before it becomes
existent just as the table must exist before it can be brown,
black, etc. This is, in fact, the gist of the criticism of the
Avicennian thesis by Averroes and Aquinas.

Avicenna was well aware of the danger that his thesis might
be misinterpreted in this way. He emphasized that we should
not confuse "existence" as an accident with ordinary accidents, like "brown," "white," etc. He emphasized that existence
is a very peculiar and unique kind of accident, for the objective reality which is referred to by a proposition like "the table
is existent" presents a completely different picture from what
is naturally suggested by the propositional form of the expression. However, Avicenna himself did not clarify the structure
of the extra-mental, objective reality which is found beyond
what is meant by the logical proposition. The problem was left
to posterity.

In the periods following Avicenna, this problem assumed
supreme importance, and a number of divergent opinions
were put forward. The philosophers belonging to the school
of thought that I am going to talk about, chose to take a
position which might look at first sight very daring or very
strange. They asserted that, in the sphere of external reality,
the proposition: "The table is existent" as understood in the
sense of substance-accident relationship turns out to be meaningless. For in the realm of external reality there is, to begin
with, no self-subsistent substance called table, nor is there a
real "accident" called "existence" to come to inhere in the

substance. The whole phenomenon of a table being qualified by "existence" turns into something like a shadow-picture, something which is not wholly illusory but which approaches the nature of an illusion. In this perspective, both the table and "existence" as its "accident" begin to look like things seen in a dream.

These philosophers do not mean to say simply that the world of reality as we perceive it in our waking experience is in itself unreal or a dream. Nor do they want to assert that the proposition: "The table is existent" does not refer to any kind of external reality. There certainly *is* a corresponding piece of reality. The only point they want to make is that the structure of external reality which corresponds to this proposition is totally different from what is normally suggested by the form of the proposition, for in this domain "existence" is the sole reality. "Table" is but an inner modification of this reality, one of its self-determinations. Thus in the realm of external reality, the subject and the predicate must exchange their places. The "table" which is the logical or grammatical subject of the proposition: "The table is existent," is in this domain not a subject; rather, it is a predicate. The real subject is "existence," while "table" is but an "accident" determining the subject into a particular thing. In fact all the so-called "essences," like being-a-table, being-a-flower, etc. are in external reality nothing but "accidents" that modify and delimit the one single reality called "existence" into innumerable things.

Such a vision of reality, however, is not accessible to human consciousness as long as it remains at the level of ordinary everyday experience. In order to have access to it, according to the philosophers of this school, the mind must experience a total transformation of itself. The consciousness must transcend the dimension of ordinary cognition where the world of being is experienced as consisting of solid, self-subsistent things, each having as its ontological core what is called essence. There must arise in the mind a totally different kind of awareness in which the world is revealed in an entirely different light. It is at this point that Iranian philosophy turns conspicuously toward mysticism. So much so that a philosopher like Mullá Sadrá comes to declare that any philosophy which is not based upon the mystical vision of reality is but a vain intellectual pastime. In more concrete terms, the basic idea here is that an integral metaphysical world view is possible only on the basis of a unique form of subject-object relationship.

It is to be remarked in this connection that, in this variety of Islamic philosophy as well as in other major philosophies of the East, metaphysics or ontology is inseparably connected with the subjective state of man, so that the self-same reality is said to be perceived differently in accordance with the different degrees of consciousness.

The problem of the unique form of subject-object relationship is discussed in Islam as the problem of *ittihád al-'álim wa-al-ma'lúm,* i.e. the "unification of the knower and the known." Whatever may happen to be the object of knowledge, the highest degree of knowledge is always achieved when the knower, the human subject, becomes completely unified and identified with the object so much so that there remains no differentiation between the two. For differentiation or distinction means distance, and distance in cognitive relationship means ignorance. As long as there remains between the subject and object the slightest degree of distinction, that is to say, as long as there are subject and object as two entities distinguishable from one another, perfect cognition is not realized. To this we must add another observation concerning the object of cognition, namely that the highest object of cognition, for the philosophers of this school, is "existence."[1] And according to Mullá Sadrá, one of the most prominent figures of this school, real knowledge of "existence" is obtainable not by rational reasoning but only through a very peculiar kind of intuition. This latter mode of cognition, in the view of Mullá Sadrá, consists precisely in knowing "existence" through the "unification of the knower and the known," i.e. knowing "existence" not from the outside as an "object" of knowledge, but from the inside, by man's *becoming* or rather *being* "existence" itself, that is, by man's self-realization. It is evident that such unification of the knower and the known cannot be realized at the level of everyday human experience where the subject stands eternally opposed to the object. The subject in such a state grasps "existence" only as an object. It objectifies "existence" as it objectifies all other things, while "existence" in its reality as *actus essendi* definitely and persistently refuses to be an "object." An objectified "existence" is but a distortion of the reality of "existence."

Haydar Ámulí, one of the foremost Iranian metaphysicians of the fourteenth century says: "When man attempts to approach "existence" through his weak intellect (*'aql da'íf*) and feeble thinking (*afkár rakíkah*), his natural blindness and perplexity go on but increasing."[2]

The common people who have no access to the transcendental experience of Reality are compared to a blind man who cannot walk safely without the help of a stick in his hand. The stick giving guidance to the blind man here symbolizes the rational faculty of the mind. The strange thing about this is that the stick upon which the blind man relies happens to be the very cause of his blindness. Only when Moses threw down his stick were the veils of the phenomenal forms removed from his sight. Only then did he witness, beyond the veils, beyond the phenomenal forms, the splendid beauty of absolute Reality.

محمود شبستری

Mahmúd Shabastarí, an outstanding Iranian mystic philosopher of the thirteenth-fourteenth centuries, says in his celebrated *Gulshan-e Ráz*:

> Throw away reason; be always with Reality,
> For the eye of the bat has no power to gaze at the sun.

لاهيجی

Reason trying to see the absolute Reality, says Láhíjí in his *Commentary on the Gulhan-e Ráz*,[3] is just like the eye trying to gaze at the sun. Even from afar, the overwhelming effulgence of the sun blinds the eye of reason. And as the eye of reason goes up to higher stages of Reality, gradually approaching the metaphysical region of the Absolute, the darkness becomes ever deeper until everything in the end turns black.

As man comes close to the vicinity of the sacred region of Reality, Muhammad Láhíjí remarks, the brilliant light issuing forth from it appears black to his eyes. Brightness at its ultimate extremity becomes completely identical with utter darkness. To use a less metaphorical terminology, "existence" in its absolute purity is to the eyes of an ordinary man as invisible as sheer nothing. Thus it comes about that the majority of men are not even aware of the "light" in its true reality. Like the men sitting in the cave in the celebrated Platonic myth, they remain satisfied with looking at the shadows cast by the sun. They see the faint reflections of the light on the screen of the so-called external world and are convinced that these reflections are the sole reality.

Haydar Ámulí, divides existence in this connection into (1) pure, absolute existence as pure light and (2) shadowy and dark existence: light *(núr)* and shadow *(zill)*. Seen through the eye of a real metaphysician, shadow also is existence. But it is not the pure reality of existence.[4]

The ontological status of the shadowy figures, i.e. the objectified forms of existence which, at the level of normal everyday experience, appear to the human consciousness as solid, self-subsistent things is, according to Mullá Sadrá, like that of a "mirage falsely presenting the image of water, while in reality it has nothing to do with water."[5] However, the phenomenal things, although they are of a shadowy nature in themselves, are not wholly devoid of reality either. On the contrary, they are real if they are considered in relation to their metaphysical source. In fact even in the empirical world, nothing is wholly unreal. Even a mirage is not altogether unreal in the sense that its perception is induced by the actual existence of a wide stretch of desert land. But in a metaphysical perspective, the desert land which is the empirical basis of a mirage must itself he regarded as something of the nature of a mirage, if it is compared with the ultimate ground of reality.

This Islamic approach to the problem of the reality and unreality of the phenomenal world will rightly remind us of the position taken by Vedanta philosophy as represented by the celebrated dictum of Shankara which runs: "The world is a continuous series of cognitions of Brahman" (*Brahma-pratya-yasantair jagat*).[6] For Shankara too, the phenomenal world is Brahman or the absolute Reality itself as it appears to the ordinary human consciousness in accordance with the natural structure of the latter. In this respect, the world is not a pure illusion, because under each of the phenomenal forms there is hidden the Brahman itself, just as a rope mistakenly perceived as a snake in darkness is not altogether unreal because the perception of the snake is here induced by the actual existence of the rope. The phenomenal world becomes unreal or false (*jagan mithyá*) only when it is taken as an ultimate, self-subsistent reality. It is not at all false and illusory *qua* Brahman as perceived by our non-absolute consciousness.[7]

Likewise in Islamic philosophy, the phenomenal world is real in so far as it is the absolute truth or Reality as perceived by the relative human mind in accordance with its natural structure. But it is false and unreal if taken as something ultimate and self-subsistent. A true metaphysician worthy of the name is one who is capable of witnessing in every single thing in the world the underlying Reality of which the phenomenal form is but a self-manifestation and self-determination. But the problem now is: How can such a vision of Reality be obtainable as a matter of actual experience? To this crucial question the Islamic philosophy of existence answers by saying that it is obtainable only through an inner witnessing" (*shuhúd*), "tasting" *(dhawq)*, "presence" *(hudúr)*, or "illumination" *(ishráq)*.

Whatever these technical terms exactly mean, and to whatever degree they may differ from one another, it will be evident in any case that such an experience of Reality cannot be actualized as long as there remains the subject of cognition as a "subject," that is to say, as long as there remains in man ego-consciousness. The empirical ego is the most serious hindrance in the way of the experience of "seeing by self-realization." For the subsistence of the individual ego places of necessity an epistemological distance between man and the reality of "existence," be it his own "existence." The reality of existence is immediately grasped only when the empirical selfhood is annihilated, when the ego-consciousness is completely dissolved into the consciousness of Reality, or rather, consciousness which *is* Reality.

Hence the supreme importance attached in this type of philosophy to the experience called *faná'*, meaning literally annihilation, that is, the total nullification of the ego-consciousness. The phenomenal world is the world of multiplicity. Although multiplicity is ultimately nothing other than the self-revealing aspect of the absolute Reality itself, he who knows Reality only in the form of multiplicity knows Reality only through its variously articulated forms, and fails to perceive the underlying unity of Reality.

The immediate experience of Reality through "self-realization," consists precisely in the immediate cognition of absolute Reality before it is articulated into different things. In order to see Reality in its absolute indetermination, the ego also must go beyond its own essential determination.

Thus it is certain that there is a human aspect to the experience of *fana'* inasmuch as it involves a conscious effort on the part of man to purify himself from all the activities of the ego. 'Abd al-Rahmán Jámí, a famous Iranian poet-philosopher of the fifteenth century, says, "keep yourself away from your own ego, and set your mind free from the vision of others."[8] The word "others" here means everything other than absolute Reality. Such efforts made by persons for the attainment of *fana'* are technically called *tawhíd,* meaning literally "making many things one" or "unification," that is, an absolute concentration of the mind in deep meditation. It consists, as Jámí explains, in man's making his mind cleansed *(takhlís)* of its relations with anything other than absolute Reality, whether as objects of desire and will or as objects of knowledge and cognition. So much so that in the end even the consciousness of his own *fana'* must disappear from his consciousness. In this sense the experience of annihilation *(fana')* involves the annihilation of annihilation *(fana'-ye fana'),* that is, the total disappearance of the consciousness of man's own disappearance.[9] For even the consciousness of *fana'* is a consciousness of something other than absolute Reality. It is significant that such an absolute *fana'* where there is not even a trace of the *fana'*-consciousness, which, be it remarked in passing, evidently finds its exact counterpart in the Mahayana Buddhist conception of *shúnyatá* or nothingness, is not regarded as merely a subjective state realized in man; it is at one and the same time the realization or actualization of absolute Reality in its absoluteness.

This point cannot be too much emphasized, for if we fail to grasp it correctly, the very structure of Islamic metaphysics would not be rightly understood. *Fanā'* is certainly a human experience. It is man who actually experiences it. But it is not solely a human experience. For when he does experience it, he is no longer himself. In this sense man is not the subject of experience. The subject is rather the metaphysical Reality itself. In other words, the human experience of *fanā'* is itself the self-actualization of Reality. It is, in Islamic terminology, the preponderance of the self-revealing aspect of Reality over its own self-concealing aspect, the preponderance of the *zāhir,* the manifest, over the *bātin,* the concealed. The experience of *fanā'* is in this respect nothing but an effusion (*fayd*) of the metaphysical light of absolute Reality.

The force of the self-revealing aspect of Reality is constantly making itself felt in the things and events of the phenomenal world. Otherwise there would be no phenomenal world around us. But there, in the phenomenal world, Reality reveals itself only through relative and spatio-temporal forms. In the absolute consciousness of a mystic metaphysician on the contrary, it reveals itself in its original absoluteness beyond all relative determinations. This is what is technically known as *kashf* or *mukāshafah,* i.e. the experience of unveiling."[10]

Fanā' as a human experience is man's experiencing the total annihilation of his own ego and consequently of all things that have been related to the ego in the capacity of its objects of cognition and volition. This experience would correspond to a spiritual event which is known in Zen Buddhism as the "mind-and-body-dropping-off" (*shin jin datsu raku*), i.e. the whole unity of "mind-body," which is no other than the so-called ego or self losing its seemingly solid ground and falling off into the bottom of metaphysical and epistemological nothingness.[11] However, neither in Zen Buddhism nor in Islam does this represent the ultimate height of metaphysical experience.

After having passed through this crucial stage, the philosopher is supposed to ascend to a still higher stage which is known in Zen as the dropped-off-mind-and-body (*datsu raku shin jin*) and in Islam as the experience of *baqá'* or "survival," i.e. eternal remaining in absolute Reality with absolute Reality. At the stage of *fana'*, the pseudo-ego or the relative self has completely dissolved into nothingness. At the next stage man is resuscitated out of the nothingness, completely transformed into an absolute Self. What is resuscitated is outwardly the same old man, but he is a man who has once transcended his own determination. He regains his normal, daily consciousness and accordingly the normal, daily, phenomenal world of multiplicity again begins to spread itself out before his eyes. The world of multiplicity appears again with all its infinitely rich colors. Since, however, he has already cast off his own determination, the world of multiplicity he perceives is also beyond all determinations.

The new world view is comparable to the world view which a drop of water might have if it could suddenly awake to the fact that being an individual self-subsistent drop of water has been but a pseudo-determination which it has imposed upon itself, and that it has in reality always been nothing other than the limitless sea. In a similar manner, the mystic-philosopher who has attained to the state of *baqá'* sees himself and all other things around him as so many determinations of one single Reality. The seething world of becoming turns in his sight into a vast field in which absolute Reality manifests itself in myriad different forms. This vision of reality has produced in Islam a typically Oriental metaphysical system based on a dynamic and delicate interplay between unity and multiplicity. I want to discuss some aspects of this problem in what follows.

At this point I would like to repeat what I have previously said: namely, that in this type of philosophy metaphysics is most closely correlated with epistemology.

The correlation between the metaphysical and the epistemological means in this context the relation of ultimate identity between what is established as the objective structure of reality and what is usually thought to take place subjectively in human consciousness. It means, in brief, that there is no distance, there should be no distance between the "subject" and "object." It is not exact enough even to say that the state of the subject essentially determines the aspect in which the object is perceived, or that one and the same object tends to appear quite differently in accordance with different points of view taken by the subject. Rather the state of consciousness *is* the state of the external world. That is to say, the objective structure of reality is no other than the other side of the subjective structure of the mind. And that precisely is the metaphysical Reality.

Thus to take up the problem of our immediate concern, *faná'* and *baqá'*, "annihilation" and "survival," are not only subjective states. They are objective states, too. The subjective and the objective are here two dimensions or two aspects of one and the same metaphysical structure of Reality.

I have already explained the subjective *faná'* and *baqa'*. As to the objective *faná'*, it is also known as the ontological stage of "unification" (*jam'*, meaning literally "gathering" or "all-things-being-put-together"), while the objective *baqa'* is called the stage of the "unification of unification" (*jam' al-jam'*), "separation after unification" (*farq ba'd al-jam'*), or "second separation" (*farq thání*). I shall first explain what is really meant by these technical terms.[12]

The word "separation" (*farq*) primarily refers to the common-sense view of reality. Before we subjectively attain to the stage of *fanâ'*, we naturally tend to separate the Absolute from the phenomenal world. The phenomenal world is the realm of relativity, a world where nothing is absolute, where all things are observed to be impermanent, transient, and constantly changing. This is the kind of observation which plays an exceedingly important role in Buddhism as the principle of universal impermanence. The world of multiplicity, be it remarked, is a realm where our senses and reason fulfil their normal functions.

Over against this plane of relativity and impermanence, the Absolute is posited as something essentially different from the former, as something which absolutely transcends the impermanent world. Reality is thus divided up into two completely different sections. This dichotomy is called "separation" (*farq*). The empirical view of reality is called "separation" also because in this view all things are separated from one another by essential demarcations. A mountain is a mountain. It is not, it cannot be, a river. Mountain and river are essentially different from one another.

The world of being appears in a completely different light when looked at through the eyes of one who has reached the subjective state of *fanâ'*. The essential demarcations separating one thing from another, are no longer here. Multiplicity is no longer observable. This comes from the fact that since there is no ego-consciousness left, that is to say, since there is no epistemological subject to see things, there are naturally no objects to be seen. As all psychological commotions and agitations become reduced to the point of nothingness in the experience of *fanā'*, the ontological commotion that has hitherto characterized the external world calms down into an absolute Stillness. As the limitation of the ego disappears on the side of the subject, all the phenomenal limitations of things in the objective world disappear from the scene, and there remains only the absolute unity of Reality in its purity as an absolute awareness prior to its bifurcation into subject and object. This stage is called in Islam "gathering" (*jam'*) because it "gathers" together all the things that constitute the phenomenal world and brings them back to their original indiscrimination. In theological terminology this is said to be the stage at which the believer witnesses God, and God alone, without seeing any creature. It is also known as the stage of "God was, and there was nothing else." This stage would correspond to what the Taoist philosopher Chuang Tzu calls "chaos" (*hun tun*).[13]

The next stage, which is the ultimate and highest, is that of *baqā'*. Subjectively, this is the stage at which man regains his phenomenal consciousness after having experienced the existential annihilation of its own self. The mind that has completely stopped working at the previous stage resumes its normal cognitive activity. Corresponding to this subjective rebirth, the phenomenal world also takes its rise again. The world once more unfolds itself before the man's eyes in the form of the surging waves of multiplicity. The things that have been "gathered up" into unity are again separated from one another as so many different entities. This is why the stage is called "separation after unification" or the "second separation."

There is, however, an important difference between the first and the second "separation." In the "first separation," which is the pre-*fanā'* stage both subjectively and objectively, the innumerable things were definitely separated from one another, each being observed only as an independent, self-subsistent entity. And, as such, they are made to stand opposed to the Absolute, again as two entirely different ontological domains between which there is no internal relationship. At the stage of the "second separation," too, all phenomenal things are unmistakably distinguished from one another through each one of them having its own essential demarcation which is peculiar to itself. And this ontological dimension of multiplicity *qua* multiplicity is also unmistakably differentiated from the dimension of unity.

The "second separation," however, is not sheer multiplicity, because at this stage all the essential demarcations of the things, although they are clearly observable, are known to be nothing other than so many self-determinations of the absolute unity itself. And since the "unity" annihilates in its own purity all ontological differences, the whole world of being is here found to be ultimately reducible to one single metaphysical root. From such a viewpoint, what can be said to exist in the real sense of the word is nothing but this unique metaphysical root of all things. In this sense the multiplicity which is observable here is unity. The only important point is that unity at this stage is unity with inner articulations. And this stage is called "gathering of gathering" (*jam' al-jam'*) for the very reason that the phenomenal things that have all been once reduced to the absolute unity of total annihilation at the stage of *fanā'*, i.e. the primary "gathering," are again "separated" and then again "gathered" together in this new vision of unity.

Thus the difference from this particular point of view between the Unity at the stage of *fanā'* i.e. "gathering" and the unity at the stage of *baqā'* or "gathering of gathering" consists in the fact that the unity at the stage of *fanā'* is a simple, absolute unity without even inner articulation, while the unity seen at the stage of the "gathering of gathering" is an internally articulated unity. And Reality as observed at this latter stage is philosophically a *coincidentia oppositorum* in the sense that unity is multiplicity and multiplicity is unity. It is based on the vision of unity in the very midst of multiplicity and multiplicity in the very midst of unity. For as Láhíjí remarks, unity or the Absolute here serves as a mirror reflecting all phenomenal things, while multiplicity or the phenomenal things fulfil the function of a countless number of mirrors, each reflecting in its own way the same Absolute a metaphor which is singularly similar to the Buddhist image of the moon reflected in a number of different bodies of water, the moon itself ever remaining in its original unity despite the fact that it is split up into many different moons as reflections.[14]

He who has reached this stage is known in the tradition of Islamic philosophy as a "man of two eyes" (*dhu al-'aynayn*). He is a man who, with his right eye, sees unity, i.e. absolute Reality, and nothing but unity, while with his left eye he sees multiplicity, i.e. the world of phenomenal things. What is more important about this type of man is that, in addition to his simultaneous vision of unity and multiplicity, he knows that these two are ultimately one and the same thing. Such being the case, he recognizes in every one of the actually existent things two different aspects: the aspect of *fanā'* and the aspect of *baqā'*. It goes without saying that the terms *fanā'* and *baqā'* are here taken in the ontological sense, although they are not unrelated to the subjective experience known respectively by the same appellations.

The aspect of *fanā'* in a thing is the aspect in which it is considered as something determined, individualized, and essentially delimited. In this aspect every existent thing is properly non-existent, a "nothing." For the "existence" it seems to possess is in reality a borrowed existence; in itself it is unreal (*bátil*) and subsists on the ground of Nothingness.

The aspect of *baqá'*, on the contrary, is the aspect in which the same thing is considered as a reality in the sense of a determined form of the Absolute, a phenomenal form in which the Absolute manifests itself. In this aspect, nothing in the world of being is unreal.

Every concretely existent thing is a peculiar combination of these negative and positive aspects, a place of encounter between the temporal and the eternal, between the finite and infinite, between the relative and the absolute. And the combination of these two aspects produces the concept of a "possible" (*mumkin*) thing. Contrary to the ordinary notion of ontological "possibility," a "possible" thing is not a purely relative and finite thing. As a locus of divine self-manifestation (*tajallí*), it has another aspect which directly connects it with absolute Reality. In every single thing, be it the meanest imaginable thing, the mystic-philosopher recognizes a determined self-manifestation of the Absolute.

This metaphysical situation is described by Mahmúd Shabastarí in his *Gulshan-e Ráz* through a combination of contradictory terms as "bright night amidst the dark daylight" (*shab-e roushan miyán-e rúz-e tárík*).[15] The "bright night" in this expression refers to the peculiar structure of Reality as it discloses itself at the stage of the subjective and objective *faná'* in which one witnesses the annihilation of all outward manifestations of Reality. It is "night" because at this stage nothing is discernible; all things have lost their proper colors and forms and sunk into the darkness of the original indiscrimination. This metaphysical "night," however, is said to be "bright" because absolute Reality in itself—that is, apart from all considerations of the limitations set by the very structure of our relative consciousness—is essentially luminous, illuminating its own self as well as all others.

The second half of the above expression reads "amidst the dark daylight." This means, first of all, that this absolute unity is revealing itself in the very midst of multiplicity, in the form of determined, relative things. In this sense and in this form, the absolute Reality is clearly visible in the external world, just as everything is visible in the daylight. However, the daylight in which all these things are revealed to our eyes is but a phenomenal daylight. The things that appear in it are in themselves of the nature of darkness and non-existence. This is why the "daylight" is said to be "dark."

These two contradictory aspects of Reality, namely, light and darkness, which are said to be observable in everything, bring us directly to the question: In what sense and to what degree are the phenomenal things real? The problem of the reality or unreality of the phenomenal world is indeed a crucial point in Islamic philosophy which definitely divides the thinkers into different classes constituting among themselves a kind of spiritual hierarchy. Haydar Ámulí in this connection proposes a triple division: (1) the common people (*'awámm*) or men of reason (*dhawu al-'aql*), (2) the privileged people (*khawáss*) or men of intuition (*dhawu al-'ayn*), and (3) the privileged of all privileged people (*khawáss al-khawáss*) or men of reason and intuition (*dhawu al-'aql wa-al-'ayn*).[16]

The lowest stage is represented by those of the first class who only see multiplicity. They are those who are firmly convinced that the things as they perceive them in this world are the sole reality, there being nothing beyond or behind it. From the viewpoint of a real mystic-philosopher, the eyes of these people are veiled by the phenomenal forms of multiplicity from the view of unity that underlies them. The phenomenal things, instead of disclosing, by their very mode of existence, Something that manifests itself through them, function as impenetrable veils obstructing the sight of that self-revealing

Something. This situation is often compared in Islamic philosophy to the state of those who are looking at images reflected in a mirror without being at all aware of the existence of the mirror. In this metaphor the mirror symbolizes absolute Reality, and the images reflected in it the phenomenal things.

Objectively speaking, even the people of this type are perceiving the images on the surface of the mirror. There would be no image perceivable without the mirror. But subjectively they believe the images to be real and self-subsistent things. The metaphor of the mirror happens to be one of those important metaphors that recur in Islamic philosophy on many different occasions. Another metaphor of this nature is the sea surging in waves, which, in the particular metaphysical context in which we are actually interested, indicates that the people notice only the rolling waves forgetting the fact that the waves are nothing but outward forms assumed by the sea. Describing how phenomenal multiplicity veils and conceals the underlying unity of Reality, Jámi says,

> Existence is a sea, with waves constantly raging,
> Of the sea the common people perceive nothing but the waves.
> Behold how out of the depth of the sea there appear innumerable waves,
> On the surface of the sea, while the sea remains concealed in the waves.[17]

I would take this opportunity to point out that Muslim philosophers tend to use metaphors and similes in metaphysics particularly in the explanation of the seemingly self-contradictory relation between unity and multiplicity, or absolute Reality and the phenomenal things. The frequent use of metaphors in metaphysics is one of the characteristic marks of

Islamic philosophy, or indeed we might say of Eastern philosophy in general. It must not be taken as a poetic ornament. A
cognitive function is definitely assigned to the use of metaphors.[18]

This may rightly remind us of Ludwig Wittgenstein's understanding of the concept of "seeing as." According to Wittgenstein,
"seeing as" involves a technique in a way which normal "seeing"
does not. Thus one might well be able to "see" but not be able to
"see as." He call this latter case "aspect-blindness."[19]

In the same way, to discover an appropriate metaphor in
the high domain of metaphysics is for Muslim philosophers a
peculiar way of thinking, a mode of cognition, for it means
discovering some subtle features in the metaphysical structure
of Reality, an aspect which, no matter how self-evident it may
be as a fact of transcendental Awareness, is so subtle and
evasive at the level of discursive thinking that human intellect
would otherwise be unable to take hold of it.

This said, we shall continue our consideration of the various
stages in metaphysical cognition. Those of the common people
who perceive nothing beyond multiplicity and for whom even
the word "phenomenon" does not make real sense have been
said to represent the lowest stage in the hierarchy. A stage
higher than this is reached, still within the confines of the
common people, by those who recognize something beyond
the phenomenal. This something-beyond is the Absolute—or
in popular terminology God—which is conceived as the Tran-
scendent. God is here represented as an absolute Other which
is essentially cut off from the phenomenal world. There is, in
this conception, no inner connection between God and the
world. There is between them only an external relationship
like creation and domination. Such people are known in Is-

lam as "men of externality" (*ahl-e záhir*), i.e. those who see only the exterior surface of Reality. Their eyes are said to be afflicted with a disease preventing them from seeing the true structure of Reality. The reference is to a disease or deformity peculiar to the eye called *hawal*. Whoever is infected with it always has a double image of whatever he sees. One single object appears to his eyes as two different things.

The second class of people are those who have attained to an immediate vision of absolute Reality in the experience of *fana'*, both in the subjective and the objective sense, that is, the total annihilation of the ego and correspondingly of all the phenomenal things that constitute the external, objective world. But the people of this class just stop at this stage and do not go any further. To state the situation in more concrete terms, these people are aware only of absolute unity. They see everywhere unity, nothing else. The whole world in their view has turned into absolute unity with no articulation and determination.

Certainly, when these people come back immediately from the experience of *fana'* to their normal consciousness, multiplicity does again become visible. But the phenomenal world is simply discarded as an illusion. In their view, the world of multiplicity has no metaphysical or ontological value because it is essentially unreal. The external objects are not "existent" in the real sense of the word. They are just floating gossamers, sheer illusions backed by no corresponding realities. Such a view is in its fundamental structure identical with the Vedantic view of the phenomenal world in its popular understanding, in which the notorious word *máyá* is taken to mean sheer illusion or illusion-producing principle.

Just as this popular understanding does gross injustice to the authentic world-view of Vedanta philosophy, the exclusive emphasis on the Absolute to the irreparable detriment of the phenomenal world in Islamic metaphysics fatally distorts the authentic view of its representatives. It is in this sense that Haydar Ámulí accuses Ismailism of disbelief and heresy.[20]

From the viewpoint of the highest mystic-philosopher, even the people of this type, when they experience the vision of the Absolute, are actually doing nothing but perceiving the Absolute as it is reflected in the phenomenal things. But dazzled by the excess of light issuing forth from the Absolute, they are not aware of the phenomenal things in which it is reflected. Just as in the case of the people of the first class, the Absolute served as the mirror reflecting upon its polished surface all the phenomenal things, so in the present case the phenomenal things serve as mirrors reflecting the Absolute. In either case, man usually takes notice of the images in the mirror, and the mirror itself remains unnoticed.

It is at the third stage, that is, at the stage of the "privileged of all privileged people" that the relation between the Absolute and the phenomenal world is correctly grasped as the *coincidentia oppositorum* of unity and multiplicity. It is, moreover, in this region that the cognitive value of metaphorical thinking to which reference has been made earlier is most profusely displayed.

Those whose consciousness has been raised to the height of *baqa'* after the experience of *faná'*, experience the relation between the Absolute and the phenomenal as the *coincidentia oppositorum* of unity and multiplicity. Theologically speaking, they are those who are able to see God in the creature and the creature in God. They can see both the mirror and the images that are reflected in it, God and the creature at this stage alternately serving as both the mirror and the image. The one selfsame "existence" is seen at once to be God and the creature, or absolute Reality and the phenomenal world, unity and multiplicity.

The sight of the multiplicity of phenomenal things does not obstruct the sight of the pure unity of ultimate Reality. Nor does the sight of unity stand in the way of the appearance of multiplicity.[21] On the contrary, the two complement each other in disclosing the pure structure of Reality. For they are the two essential aspects of Reality, unity representing the aspect of "absoluteness" (*itláq*) or "comprehensive contraction" (*ijmál*), and multiplicity the aspect of "determination" (*taqyid*) or "concrete expansion" (*tafsíl*). Unless we grasp in this way unity and multiplicity in a single act of cognition we are not having a whole integral view of Reality as it really is. Haydar Ámulí calls such a simultaneous intuition of the two aspects of Reality the "unification of existence" (*tawhíd wujúdí*) and regards it as the sole authentic philosophical counterpart of religious monotheism.[22] The "unification of existence" thus understood consists in a fundamental intuition of the one single reality of "existence" in everything without exception. In the Absolute, which corresponds theologically to God, it sees "existence" in its absolute purity and unconditionality, while in the things of the phenomenal world it recognizes the concrete differentiations of the selfsame reality of "existence" in accordance with its own inner articulations. Philosophically this is the position generally known as "oneness of existence" (*wahdat al-wujúd*), which is an idea of central importance going back to Ibn 'Arabi.

The particular type of metaphysics based on this kind of existential intuition begins with the statement that the Absolute only is real, that the Absolute is the sole reality, and that, consequently, nothing else is real. The differentiated world of multiplicity is therefore essentially "non-existent" (*'adam*). To this initial statement, however, is immediately added another; namely, that it does not in any way imply that the differentiated world is a void, an illusion, or sheer nothing. The ontological status of phenomenal things is rather that of relations, that is, the various and variegated relational forms of the Absolute itself. In this sense, and in this sense only, they are all real.

The rise of the phenomenal world as we actually observe it, is due primarily to two seemingly different causes which are in reality perfectly co-ordinated with each other: one metaphysical, another epistemological. Metaphysically or ontologically, the phenomenal world arises before our eyes because the Absolute has in itself essential, internal articulations that are called *shu'ún* (sg. *sha'n*) meaning literally "affairs," i.e. internal modes of being. They are also called existential "perfections" (*kamálát*), a conception similar in an important and significant way to Lao Tzu's idea of "virtues" (*té*) in relation to the way (*tao*).[23] These internal articulations naturally call for their own externalization. As a consequence, "existence" spreads itself out in myriads of self-determinations.

Epistemologically, on the other hand, this act of self-determination on the part of Reality is due to the inherent limitations of the finite human consciousness. The Absolute or pure "existence" in itself is sheer unity. The Absolute remains in its original unity in no matter how many different forms it may manifest itself. In this sense the world of multiplicity is essentially of the very nature of the Absolute; it is the Absolute itself. But the original unity of the Absolute appears to the finite human consciousness as differentiated into countless finite things because of the finitude of the consciousness. The phenomenal world is the Absolute that has hidden its real formless form under the apparent forms which are caused by the very limitations inherent in the epistemological faculties of man.

The process here described of the appearance of the originally undifferentiated metaphysical unity in many different forms is called in Islamic philosophy the "self-manifestation" (*tajallí*) of "existence." The conception of the *tajallí* is structurally identical with the Vedantic conception of *adhyása* or "superimposition," according to which the originally undivided unity of pure *nirguna Brahman*, the absolutely unconditioned Absolute, appears divided because of the different "names and forms" (*náma-rúpa*) that are imposed upon the Absolute by "ignorance" (*avidyá*). It is remarkable, from the viewpoint of comparison between Islamic philosophy and Vedanta, that *avidyá* which, subjectively, is the human "ignorance" of the true reality of things, is, objectively, exactly the same thing as *máyá* which is the self-conditioning power inherent in Brahman itself. The "names and forms" that are said to be superimposed upon the Absolute by *avidyá* would correspond to the Islamic concept of "quiddities" (*máhiyát*, sg. *máhíyah*) which are nothing other than the externalized forms of the Divine "names and attributes" (*asmá' wa-sifát*). And the Vedantic *máyá* as the self-determining power of the Absolute would find its exact Islamic counterpart in the concept of the Divine "existential mercy" (*rahmah wujúdíyah*).

However, even at the stage of self-manifestation, the structure of Reality as seen through the eyes of a real mystic-philosopher looks diametrically opposed to the same Reality as it appears to the relative consciousness of an ordinary man. For in the eyes of an ordinary man representing the common-sense view of things, the phenomena are the visible and manifest while the Absolute is the hidden. But in the unconditioned consciousness of a real mystic-philosopher, it is always and everywhere the Absolute that is manifest while the phenomena remain in the background.

This peculiar structure of Reality in its self-manifesting aspect (*tajallí*) is due to what I have repeatedly pointed above; namely, that the differentiated world of phenomena is not self-subsistently real. No phenomenal thing has in itself a real ontological core. The idea corresponds to the celebrated Buddhist denial of *svabháva* or "self-nature" to anything in the world. In this sense, the philosophical standpoint of the school of the "oneness of existence" (*wahdat al-wujúd*) is most obviously anti-essentialism. All so-called "essences" or "quiddities" are reduced to the position of the fictitious. The utmost degree of reality recognized to them is that of "borrowed existence." That is to say, the "quiddities" exist because they happen to be so many intrinsic modifications and determinations of the Absolute which alone can be said to exist in the fullest sense of the word.

In reference to the ontological status of the phenomenal world and its relation to the Absolute, the Muslim philosophers here proposed a number of illuminating metaphors. In view of the above-mentioned importance of metaphorical thinking in Islam, I shall give here a few of them. Thus Mahmúd Shabastarí says in the *Gulshan-e Ráz*:

> The appearance of all things "other" [than the Absolute]
> is due to your imagination [i.e. the structure of human
> cognition],
> Just as a swiftly turning point appears as a circle.[24]

Concerning these verses Láhíjí makes the following observation. The appearance of the world of multiplicity as something "other" than the Absolute is due to the working of the faculty of imagination which is based on sense perception and which is by nature unable to go beyond the phenomenal surface of the things. In truth, there is only one single Reality manifesting itself in a myriad of different forms. But in this domain sense perception is utterly untrustworthy. For it is liable to see a mirage as something really existent when it is in truth non-existent. It sees drops of rain falling from the sky as straight lines. A man sitting in a boat tends to think that the shore is moving while the ship stands still."[25] When in the dark a firebrand is turned very swiftly, we naturally perceive a burning circle. What is really existent in this case is the firebrand as a single point of fire. But the swift circular movement makes the point of fire appear as a circle of light. Such, Láhíjí argues, is the relation between the Absolute, whose state of unity is comparable to a point of fire, and the world of multiplicity, which in its essential constitution resembles the circle produced by the movement of the point.[26] In other words, the phenomenal world is a trace left behind by the incessant creative acting of the Absolute.

The philosophical problem here is the ontological status of the circle of light. Evidently the circle does not "exist" in the fullest sense of the word. It is in itself false and unreal. It is equally evident, however, that the circle cannot be said to be sheer nothing. It does exist in a certain sense. It is real as far as it appears to our consciousness and also as far as it is produced by the point of fire which is really existent on the empirical level of our experience. The ontological status of all phenomenal things that are observable in this world is essentially of such a nature.

Another interesting metaphor that has been proposed by Muslim philosophers is that of ink and different letters written with it.[27] Letters written with ink do not *really* exist *qua* letters. For the letters are but various forms to which meanings have been assigned through convention. What really and concretely exists is nothing but ink. The "existence" of the letters is in truth no other than the "existence" of the ink which is the sole, unique reality that unfolds itself in many forms of self-modification. One has to cultivate, first of all, the eye to see the selfsame reality of ink in all letters, and then to see the letters as so many intrinsic modifications of the ink.

The next metaphor—that of the sea and waves—is probably more important in that, firstly, it is shared by a number of non-Islamic philosophical systems of the East and is, therefore, apt to disclose one of the most basic common patterns of thinking in the East; and that, secondly, it draws attention to an extremely important point that has not been made clear by the preceding metaphors; namely, that the Absolute, in so far as it is the Absolute, cannot really dispense with the phenomenal world, just as the "existence" of the phenomenal world is inconceivable except on the basis of the "existence" of the Absolute, or more properly, the "existence" which is the Absolute itself.

Of course, the Absolute can be conceived by the intellect as being beyond all determinations, and as we have seen earlier, it can even be intuited as such, in its eternal unity and absolute unconditionality. We can go even a step further and conceive it as something beyond the condition of unconditionality itself.[28]

But such a view of the Absolute is an event that takes place only in our consciousness. In the realm of extra-mental reality, the Absolute cannot even for a single moment remain without manifesting itself.

As Haydar Ámulí says, "the sea, as long as it is the sea, cannot separate itself from the waves; nor can the waves subsist independently of the sea. Moreover, when the sea appears in the form of a wave, the form cannot but be different from the form of another wave, for it is absolutely impossible for two waves to appear in one and the same place under one single form."[29]

Haydar Ámulí recognizes in this peculiar relationship between the sea and the waves an exact image of the ontological relationship between the stage of undifferentiated "existence" and the stage of the differentiated world. He remarks:

> Know that absolute existence or God is like a limitless ocean, while the determined things and individual existents are like innumerable waves or rivers. Just as the waves and rivers are nothing other than the unfolding of the sea according to the forms required by its own perfections which it possesses qua water as well as by its own peculiarities which it possesses *qua* sea, so are the determined existents nothing other than the unfolding of absolute existence under those forms that are required by its own essential perfections as well as by its peculiarities belonging to it as its inner articulations.
>
> Further, the waves and rivers are *not* the sea in one respect, while in another they are the same thing as the sea. In fact, the waves and rivers are different from the sea in respect of their being determined and particular. But they are not different from the sea in respect of their own essence and reality, namely, from the point of view of their being pure water. In exactly the same way, the determined existents are different from the Absolute in their being determined and conditioned, but they are not different from it in respect of their own essence and reality which is pure existence. For from this latter viewpoint, they are all nothing other than existence itself.[30]

It is interesting that Haydar Ámulí goes on to analyze this ontological situation from a kind of semantic point of view. He says:

The sea, when it is determined by the form of the wave, is called waves. The selfsame water, when determined by the form of the river, is called a river, and when determined by the form of the brook, is called a brook. In the same way it is called rain, snow, ice, etc.. In reality, however, there is absolutely nothing but sea or water, for the wave, river, brook, etc. are merely names indicating the sea. In truth (i.e. in its absolutely unconditioned reality) it bears no name; there is nothing whatsoever to indicate it. No, it is a matter of sheer linguistic convention even to designate it by the word sea itself.[31]

And he adds that exactly the same is true of "existence" or "reality."

There are still other famous metaphors such as that of the mirror and the image, and that of one and the numbers which are formed by the repetition of one. All of them are important in that each one throws light on some peculiar aspect of the relation between unity and multiplicity which is not clearly revealed by others.

The most important conclusion to be drawn from a careful consideration of the metaphors that have just been given is that there are recognizable in the metaphysical Reality or the Absolute itself two different dimensions. In the first of these dimensions, which is metaphysically the ultimate stage of Reality, the Absolute is the Absolute in its absoluteness, that is, in its absolute indetermination. It corresponds to the Vedantic concept of the *parabrahman*, the "Supreme Brahman" and to the neo-Confucian idea of the *wu chi*, the "Ultimateless." Both in Vedanta and Islam, the Absolute at this supreme stage is not even God, for after all "God" is but a determination of the Absolute, in so far at least as it differentiates the Absolute from the world of creation.

In the second of the two domains, the Absolute is still the Absolute, but it is the Absolute in relation to the world. It is the Absolute considered as the ultimate source of the phenomenal world, as Something which reveals itself in the form of multiplicity. It is only at this stage that the name—Allâh in Islam—becomes applicable to the Absolute. It is the stage of *parameshvara*, the supreme Lord in Vedanta, and in the neo-Confucian world-view the position of the *t'ai chi*, the "Supreme Ultimate" which is no other than the *wu chi*, the "Ultimate of Nothingness" as an eternal principle of creativity.

Such is the position generally known as oneness of existence (*wahdat al-wujúd*) which exercised a tremendous influence on the formative process of the philosophic as well as poetic mentality of Iranian Muslims, and whose basic structure I wanted to explain in this first essay. It will be clear by now that it is a serious mistake to consider—as it has often been done—this position as pure monism or even as "existential monism." For it has evidently an element of dualism in the sense that it recognizes two different dimensions of reality in the metaphysical structure of the Absolute. Nor is it of course right to regard it as dualism, for the two different dimensions of reality are *ultimately,* i.e., in the form of *coincidentia oppositorum*, one and the same thing. The "oneness of existence" is neither monism nor dualism. As a metaphysical vision of Reality based on a peculiar existential experience, which consists in seeing unity in multiplicity and multiplicity in unity, it is something far more subtle and dynamic than philosophical monism or dualism.

It is interesting to observe, moreover, that such a view of Reality, considered as a bare structure, is not at all exclusively Iranian. It is, on the contrary, commonly shared more or less by many of the major philosophical schools of the East. The important point is that this basic common structure is variously colored in such a way that each school or system differs from others by the emphasis it places on certain particular aspects of the structure and also by the degree to which it goes in dwelling upon this or that particular major concept. Now, by further elaborating the conceptual analysis of the basic structure, taking into consideration at the same time the major differences which are found between various systems, we might hopefully arrive at a comprehensive view of at least one of the most important types of Eastern philosophy which may further be fruitfully compared with a similar type of philosophy in the West. It is my conviction that a real, deep, philosophical understanding between the East and West becomes possible only on the basis of a number of concrete rsearch works of this nature conducted in various fields of philosophy both Western and Eastern.

NOTES

1. Cf. Mullá Sadrá, *al-Shawáhid ai-Rubúbíyah,* ed. Jalál al-Dín Áshtiyání (Mashhad, 1967), 14.

2. Cf. his *Risálah Nadq al-Nuqúd,* ed. Henry Corbin and Osman Yahya (Tehran-Paris, 1969), 625.

3. Muhammad Láhíjí, *Sharh-e Gulshan-e Ráz* (Tehran, 1337 A.H.), 94-97.

4. Cf. Jámi', *al-Asrár wa-Manba' al-Anwár,* ed. Henry Corbin and Osman Yahya (Tehran-Paris, 1969), 259, 261.

5. Cf. Mullá Sadrá, *al-Shawáhid al-Rubúbíyah,* 448.

6. *Vivecarudamani,* 521.

7. S. N. L. Shrivastava, *Samkara and Bradley* (New Delhi, 1968), 45-47.

8. *Lawá'ih,* ed. M. H. Tasbíhí (Tehran, 1342 A.H.), 19.

9. Ibid., 19.

10. Nihat Keklik, *Sadreddin Konevi'nin Felsefesinde Allah, Káinát ve Insan* (Istanbul, 1967), 6-9.

11. This and the following expression: *datsu' raku shin jin* appearing in the next paragraph belong to the technical terminology of the celebrated Japanese Zen master Dógen (1200-1253 C.E.).

12. The following description is an elaboration of what Láhíjí says about these technical terms in his *Sharh-e Gulshan-e Ráz* ("Commentary on the *Gulshan-e Ráz*"), 26-27.

13. For an analysis of the Confucian concept of "chaos" see my essay, "The Archetypal Image of Chaos in Chuang Tzu: The Problem of the Mythopoeic Level of Discourse, *Celestial Journey: Far Eastern Ways of Thinking* (Ashland, Oregon: White Cloud Press, 1995).

14. The same metaphor is very frequently used for a similar purpose in Oriental philosophy. Thus, to give one more example, Chu Tzu, (1130-1200 C.E.), a famous Confucian philosopher of the Sung dynasty, remarks, on the problem of how the Supreme Ultimate (*t'ai chi*) is related to its manifestations in the physical world, that the Supreme Ultimate in relation to multiplicity is just like the moon which is reflected in many rivers and lakes and is visible everywhere without being really divided up into many. (Cf. *Chu Tzú Yü Lei*, Book 94).

15. *Gulshan-e Ráz*, v. 127, 100. Cf. Láhíjí's Commentary, 101. See chapter two of this book for a fuller discussion of light and darkness in Shabestarí's *Gulshan-e Ráz*.

16. Ámulí, *Jámi' al-Asrár*, p. 113. 591.

17. *Lawá'ih*, 61.

18. On the distinction between the ornamental and the cognitive function of metaphors, see Marcus B. Hester, *The Meaning of Poetic Metaphor*, (The Hague-Paris, 1967), Introduction.

19. Ludwig Wittgenstein, *Philosophical Investigations*. Translated by G.E.M. Anscombe (New York: MacMillan, 1953), 213.

20. Ámulí, *Jami' al-Asrár*, 217, 221.

21. Ibid., 113.

22. Ibid., 113-115.

23. Cf. my *Sufism and Taoism: Key Philosophic Concepts* (Berkeley: University of California Press, 1983), 358-367.

24. *Gulshan-e Ráz*, v. 15, 19.

25. An interesting correspondence is recorded in the writings of Zen master Dógen, commenting on the same situation in his *Shóbógenzó* (III, *Gen Jó Kó An*): "If a man on board a ship turns his eyes toward the shore, he erroneously thinks that it is the shore that is moving. But if he examines his ship, he realizes that it is the ship that is moving on. Just in a similar way, if man forms for himself a false view of his own ego and considers on that basis the things in the world, he is liable to have a mistaken view of his own mind-nature as if it were a self-subsistent entity. If, however, he comes to know the truth of the matter through immediate experience (corresponding to the experience of *faná'* in Islam) and goes back to the very source of all things (corresponding to the Islamic idea of 'existence' in its original state of Unity), he will clearly notice that the ten thousand things (i.e. all phenomenal things) are ego-less (i.e. have no self-subsistence)."

26. Láhíjí, *Sharh-e Gulshan-e Ráz*, , 19.

27. Ámulí, *Jámi' al-Asrár*, 106-107.

28. This is known as the stage at which "existence" is conceived as *lá bi-shart maqsami*, i.e. an absolute unconditionality in which "existence" is conceived as not being determined even by the quality of being-unconditional, The stage corresponds to what Lao Tzu calls the "Mystery of Mysteries" *(hsüan chih yu hsüan)* and what Chuang Tzu designates by the repetition of the word *wu* or "non-existence", i.e., *wu wu*, meaning "non-non-existence."

29. Ámulí, *Jámi' al-Asrár*, 161-162.

30. Ibid., 206-207.

31. Ibid., 207-209.

CHAPTER 2

THE PARADOX OF
LIGHT AND DARKNESS
IN THE GARDEN MYSTERY
OF SHABASTARÍ

Inna li-Alláh sab'ín alf hijáb min núr wa-zulmah

Verily, God is hidden behind seventy thousand veils of
Light and Darkness

I

THIS ESSAY, a study of the structure of metaphorical thinking in Iranian Sufism, will trace this type of thinking back to its experiential origin, that is to say, by observing the very process by which archetypal metaphors arise out of the transcendental awareness of Reality. The study will analyze, for this particular purpose, two of the key metaphors of Sufism, light (*núr*) and darkness (*zulmah*) in their paradoxical interactions, as they appear in the *Gulsham-e Ráz* of Mahmúd Shabastarí and as they are philosophically explicated by Muhammad Láhíjí in his celebrated commentary upon this poem.

Mahmúd Shabastarí is one of the most famous Persian mystic-philosophers, or "theosophers," of the fourteenth century (d. 1320 C.E.). His *Gulshan-e Ráz,* or the *Garden of Mystery,* is a long philosophic poem which is not only a unanimously recognized masterpiece of Shabastarí's, but is also given a very high place in the history of Persian literature.

The importance of the *Garden of Mystery* has induced a number of distinguished thinkers to write commentaries upon it, the most important of which is the *Mafátíh al-I'júz fí Sharh-e Gulshan-e Ráz*[1] by Láhíjí, whose thought I shall examine in the following, together with that of Shabastarí himself. Muhammad Gíláni Láhíjí (d. probably 1506–7 C.E.) was an outstanding Sufi master of the dervish order called Núrbakhshíyah, and the most famous of the successors of the master Núrbakhsh (d. 1465 C.E.). His commentary has been studied for centuries not only as the best commentary upon the *Garden of Mystery,* but also as one of the most lucid, systematic expositions of Sufi philosophy written in Persian.[2]

II

As a convenient starting point for the discussion of our problem, let us begin by inspecting the classical definition of metaphor given by Aristotle in his *Poetics.* It runs: "Metaphor consists in giving the thing a name that belongs to something else; the transference being either from genus to species, or from species to genus, or from species to species, or on grounds of analogy."[3] Of the various possible forms of semantic transference mentioned here by Aristotle, it is in modern times the last one, namely the transference based on the observation of analogy, that is usually thought of when one speaks of metaphors.[4]

Thus, in accordance with this understanding, we may say that a metaphor is a linguistic sign which has a proper, conventionally established reference to a thing [A] being used in reference to something else [B] on the ground of some structural similarity observed between A and B. That is to say, we have a metaphor whenever a word is used in a double role, pointing at the same time to two different things [A and B], the first being its literal or conventional meaning and the second its non-conventional or figurative meaning. As Paul Henle says: "A word is an *immediate sign* of its literal sense and a *mediate* sign of its figurative sense."[5]

If such is the correct understanding of "metaphor," the Sufi use of the word light (*núr*), for example, clearly constitutes a metaphor. For in the particular context of Sufi terminology, the word light still retains its literal sense, which it indicates in ordinary, daily circumstances: physical light. But it refers at the same time to a certain unusual spiritual experience peculiar to a certain phase of mystic life, and there is—at least from the subjective viewpoint of the Sufi who experiences it—an undeniable structural analogy between the two experiences.

However, again from the subjective viewpoint of the Sufi who actually uses the word light in reference to some aspects of his transcendental experience of Reality, the whole thing would appear as highly problematic. The problem of metaphor, in other words, is for him not as simple as might be imagined from the Aristotelian definition of it. For the Sufi, to begin with, is firmly convinced that if there is at all anything in the world that might be fully entitled to be called light, it is the spiritual light as he experiences it, not the physical counterpart of it. Physical light, even the light of the sun, let alone artificial light, is for him too weak to be real. So overwhelmingly strong is the light which he sees with his "eye of spiritual vision" (*'ayn al-basírah*). Compared with the latter kind of light, the physical light can be called "light" only as a figure of speech. The Illuminationist (*ishráqí*) metaphysics of Suhrawardí[6] provides a remarkable example of philosophizing on the basis of the spiritual light as experienced by the mystics as the supreme metaphysical reality.

Thus, linguistically speaking, we are here in the presence of an unusual case in which the so-called literal meaning of a word turns into a figurative meaning, while what is ordinarily taken as figurative or metaphorical is found to be "real." In this particular context, the word light functions as an *immediate sign* for the spiritual light and as a *mediate sign* for the physical. So much so that from a linguistic point of view we might even say that the very occurrence of semantic transformation of such a nature in human consciousness marks the birth of a real mystic.

Obviously, then, at the very source of this kind of unusual use of words there is an original intuition of Reality. From this original intuition there develops an original form of thinking. The latter is clearly typified in Sufi poetry and philosophy. In reference to this phenomenon, it is often said that the poets and mystics express or describe the contents of their intuition by means of metaphors. This observation is certainly right in so far as it is made from the standpoint of ordinary language usage. For the word light coming out of the mouth of a mystic, for example, *is* a metaphor from such a point of view. But we have already established above that this is after all nothing but an outsider's view. Seen from the inside, that is, in terms of the inner structure of the transcendental consciousness, the so-called metaphor used by the mystic is not a metaphor in the ordinary sense of the word.

In order to have a real insight into the matter we must keep in mind the following point: it is not the case that an extraordinary vision comes first to a mystic, and that then he tries to describe it through a metaphor or a series of metaphors. Quite the contrary, the vision *is* itself the metaphor or metaphors. There is no discrepancy here between the level of the original vision and the level of its metaphorical expression. There is in this respect no room for free choice for the mystic with regard to the "metaphor" to be used. When a mystic uses the word light, for example, in describing his vision of Reality, he has not chosen it for himself from among a number of possible metaphors. Rather, the metaphor has forced itself upon him, for light is simply the concrete form in which he sees Reality. It is but natural that such a state of affairs should develop in the mystic a very peculiar thought pattern, if it is to formulate itself verbally in the dimension of the intellectual and philosophical activity of the mind. It is this kind of pattern that the present paper intends to analyze under the name of "metaphorical thinking in mysticism."

III

It is to be remarked that the pattern of thoughts typical of mystical philosophy originates in an experience known to the Islamic mystics as the stages of *fanā'*, "annihilation," and *baqā'*, "survival," an ontological and metaphysical experience of an extraordinary but neatly delineated nature, which occurs at the transcendental level of awareness.[7] And the philosophical thinking here in question evolves out of a fundamental metaphysical vision which is an immediate product of the *fanā'-baqā'* experience.

At the stage of *fanā* there is absolutely no consciousness of anything whatsoever—no object to be seen, no ego to see—not even the awareness of there being nothing. So naturally there is at this stage no possibility for the emergence of an image.

At the stage of *baqá'*, however, as the mind awakes to the existence of things—including the perceiving subject itself—and begins to resume its normal functioning, various images tend to emerge in the consciousness. These images, especially the most archetypal of them, are not for the Sufi mere subjective illusions or phantasms. They are, on the contrary, so many objective forms in which Reality discloses itself, hence the great importance attached to the basic function of imagery in the evolvement of thought in Islamic mysticism. In fact, thinking in and through images is in this context almost the only authentic form of thinking. For an image here is not a symbol indicating something beyond itself; rather, it is the indicator of its own self. It *is* a reality. Looked at from the outside, however, this type of thinking cannot but appear as "symbolic" and "metaphorical."

The images of light and darkness are constantly met with in the writings of Sufis, whether in prose or poetry. They are among the most representative of the archetypal images of Sufism in the sense that they are natural, immediate self-expressions of a root experience of the absolute Reality. The root experience—the basic structure of which will be made clear as we proceed—manifests itself most naturally in the form of the light-darkness imagery. The images themselves form an integral part of the root experience. They are not symbols by means of which Sufis try to express something entirely different. They are not metaphors as normally understood, although in fact they *are* metaphors from the viewpoint of common sense and ordinary language. If we want to place emphasis on this latter aspect of the matter, we may call the root experience itself a "metaphorical experience" in the sense that light and darkness are basically and originally there as two of its constituent factors.

Within the framework of metaphysical thinking peculiar to the school to which Shabastarí and Láhíjí belong, the Absolute or Reality at its highest stage is conceived as "pure existence." What is conceived metaphysically as existence (*wujúd*) coincides with what is grasped in terms of the root experience as light (*núr*). In this context existence *is* light. It is not the case that there is a reality called existence which bears striking similarities with light as we know it in the empirical world and which, therefore, is properly to be indicated by the metaphor of light.

The theosophic position taken by Suhrawardí the Illuminationist shows this point in the most conspicuous form. Suhrawardí places exclusive emphasis on the light as a root experience. From such a point of view, the very conception of light *as* existence deprives the fundamental experience of its fundamentality and rationalizes it into something abstract. Thus in his view *existence* is nothing but a rational "metaphor" for light. *Existence,* in short, is for him an abstract concept which the human intellect has fabricated. This Suhrawardian position is known in the history of Persian thought as the *i'tibáríyah,* "fictitiousness" or ultimate unreality, of existence.

On the contrary, in the school of the unity of existence (*wahdat al-wujúd*), supported by Shabastarí and Láhíjí, emphasis is laid on existence. They readily admit that the absolute reality as a matter of immediate experience is certainly light. But, they argue, when one remembers the ontological plenitude which one feels in this kind of experience, one cannot but take the position that the light is existence itself. In fact, even as a matter of immediate experience there is absolutely no discrepancy between *light* and *existence.* Rather, existence is a "luminous reality" (*haqíqah núráníyah*); it is itself a reality of the very nature of light. Thus it comes about that in this school the word light is often used as if it were a metaphor for existence. In reality, however, even in this school, *light* is only seemingly a metaphor.

IV

In the matter that has preceded, one point stands out as deserving special attention before we set out to analyze the paradox of light and darkness. This paradox, when elaborated rationally, will inevitably result in an ontological *coincidentia oppositorum* of unity and multiplicity. It will take on the form of a very peculiar paradoxical relationship of identity in the character of the distinction between the Absolute and phenomenal things. Thus it would appear as if the paradox of light and darkness were a "metaphorical" presentation of the ontological *coincidentia oppositorum*. In truth, however, it is the former that is the basis while the latter is but a philosophical elaboration of the former.

The very first opposition of light and darkness which we encounter in Shabastarí and Láhíjí's theosophic world view is that between absolute existence (*hastí-ye mutlaq*)[8] and the phenomenal world. As is clear from what has been said earlier, absolute existence is the same as absolute light (*núr-e mutlaq*),[9] so all phenomenal things are relegated to the region of darkness (*zulmah*). The phenomenal world is the world of our ordinary empirical experience, the world of multiplicity, the ontological dimension in which an infinite number of things seem to exist self-subsistently, being distinguished one from the other by their own essential demarcations.

This world of multiplicity is darkness in two different senses. First it is darkness in the sense that it is *in itself* nothing

and nonexistence ('adam). Because of this fundamental nothingness ('adamíyat-e aslí),[10] the world and all individual things
in the world remain forever in darkness; the word "fundamental" (aslí) in the above phrase means that nothingness is
woven into the essential structure of the phenomenal world
and is therefore never separable from it.

It is this aspect of mutliplicity that Shabastarí refers to by
the word "black-facedness" (siyah-rú'í). "No phenomenal
thing," he says, "whether in the external world or in the internal, ever leaves the state of black-facedness."[11] The expression
"black-faced" is an apt metaphor for the purely negative aspect
of all phenomenal things. Everything in this empirical world is
"black-faced." Everything is literally "nothing" and is therefore in an extremely low position. Note that "black-facedness"
is a metaphor in the ordinary sense of the word; it is not an
archetypal metaphor like light and darkness.

Since there is no intermediary ontological state conceivable between existence and nonexistence, and since,
moreoever, existence is the Absolute, it is only natural that the
world of phenomenal things, as something different and distinguishable from the Absolute—for the phenomenal world is
not the Absolute—should be nonexistence.[12] Every phenomenal thing is in this respect sheer "non-thing" (lá-shay'). The
world is naturally experienced by the mystic as a field of pure
darkness.

We have just said that every phenomenal thing is "nothing" insofar as it is something distinguishable from the
Absolute, insofar as it is "other" (ghayr) than the Absolute. In
truth it is this qualification ("insofar as . . .") that is going to
play a crucial role in the paradox of light and darkness. It is
the very beginning of this ontological paradox.

Certainly everything in the phenomenal world is, essentially speaking, nothing and is therefore darkness. That, however, does not exhaust the whole structure of a phenomenal thing. For *in a nonessential way,* everything in this world is "something." Otherwise there would be no perception, be it even an illusion, of a *phenomenal* thing.

The phenomenal world of multiplicity is essentially sheer darkness. But there is at the same time a certain respect in which this fundamental darkness turns into an apparent light. The world is light. Otherwise expressed, darkness phenomenally appears as light. This is the first paradox which we run into in our factual encounter with the world of Being.

The empirical world, insofar as it is phenomenally apparent to our senses, must be said to be a region of light. All things in fact loom up out of their original darkness in the dim light of existence. They do exist, and to that extent they are illuminated. But theirs is a dim light because it is not the light of their own; it is a borrowed light, a feeble reflection coming from the real Source of light. As Shabastarí observes, "The whole world becomes apparent by the light of the Absolute."[13]

It is imortant for our purpose to observe the highly paradoxical nature of the verse just quoted. "The whole world"—that is the world of multiplicity which, as we have already seen, is in itself sheer darkness—"becomes apparent"—becomes illumined and thereby turns into light—"by the Light of the Absolute." This means that the very darkness of the phenomenal world is a product of light, and that, paradoxically enough, the very coming-into-being of the darkness constitutes by itself the birth of the phenomenal light.

The whole process will best be understood in terms of the metaphysics of the unity of existence (*wahdat al-wujúd*) which is the result of a philosophical systematization of the fundamental experience of light and darkness. We must remark first of all that light in this context is not a stable thing, that it is, on the contrary, the incessant *act* of the effusion of creative energy from the ultimate source, which is the Absolute which, again, is pure existence. From this ultimate source the light of existence (*núr-e wujúd*) is incessantly being effused in the form of the self-manifestations (*tajallíyát*) of the Absolute. From this point of view, the phenomenal things are but determined and limited forms of the one single all-comprehensive light of existence. "Existence which is observable in this world is but a derivation and reflection of the Light of Existence which is the Absolute."[14] In this sense every phenomenal thing, being in itself a nonreality and darkness, *is* a reality and light. Thus the emergence of darkness *eo ipso* marks the emergence of light.

V

The fact that the phenomenal world is in itself sheer darkness is not apparent to the physical eye. Quite the contrary, man ordinarily and naturally tends to see the phenomenal world as light: nothing else is visible to him. The truth is that the phenomenal light is visible to the physical eye as light simply because it is an extremely feeble light, because instead of being pure, it is a mere reflection, a reflected image. Light in its absolute purity is too brilliant to be visible. It dazzles the eye; it is darkness. This is another paradox of light and darkness, the real structure of which will be clarified later on.

The phenomenal light, because of its being a reflection, is often called in Islamic mysticism *zill*, "shadow." It is a shadow cast by the sun of Reality upon the reflecting surface of nonexistence. "Just as a shadow becomes visible by the activity of Light, and just as it is a non-thing if considered in itself without any reference to its source, so does the world become apparent by the Light of real Existence; it is a non-thing and

Darkness if considered in its own essence."[15] The underlying idea is that it is only through the shadow, indirectly, that man can see pure light. But what is more relevant to our immediate topic is that man is actually far from having even this kind of indirect perception of pure light.

The phenomenal world is visible, we have said, because of its reduced light. But precisely because it is so clearly visible to us it tends to act as an insulating screen between our sight and what lies beyond it. This is the second sense in which the world of multiplicity is said to be darkness. It is darkness because it casts a black veil (hijáb) over the light of Reality. We are here confined in the region of the "darkness of multiplicity" (táríkí-ye kathrat). We see multiplicity, only multiplicity; we cannot see the absolute unity of existence hidden behind the impenetrable veil of multiplicity. Our sight stops at the phenomenal surface of the things. This idea is poetically expressed by Shabastarí in this verse: "Under the veil of every single atom there is hidden the enlivening beauty of the face of the Beloved."[16] The human tragedy is that most men are not aware even of the hidden presence of the Beloved behind the curtain.

Briefly restated in ontological terms, the whole situation at this stage will be somewhat as follows. Everything in this world is, as we have repeatedly pointed out, essentially and it itself "nothing." But insofar as everything is a determined form in which existence manifests itself, it is a reality. Everything thus has two "faces," negative and positive. In its negative aspect, it is perishable and perishing; it is fundamentally ephemeral. In its positive aspect it is imperishable and ever-lasting. The Qur'ánic verse, "All things are perishable, except His Face,"[17] is often interpreted by the mystics in this sense. Says Láhíjí: "Every phenomenal thing has two faces. Its face of non-existence (wajh-e nístí) is forever perishing, while its face

49

of existence (*wajh-e hastí*) forever remaining."[18]

But here again we come across an ontological paradox. The paradox consists in the fact that of these two "faces" it is the ephemeral and perishable (which is in itself "nothing") that appears to man's eyes as "something" solidly established on the ground of existence. The negative protrudes itself as if it were the positive. And that which is really positive is completely lost sight of. The positive aspect of a thing in which it is a self-manifestation and self-determination of absolute existence (that is, absolute light) sinks into darkness. For as long as man sees a thing as a "thing," man can never see the Thing that lies behind it.

The idea of the veil, however, is in reality of a more complicated structure, because it contains in itself other basic paradoxes. One of them is the following. We have just said that the phenomenal world works as an impenetrable veil concealing the Absolute behind it; the Absolute is not visible because of the veil. But on reflection we easily discover that this is a very inexact description of the real ontrological situation. For as we have seen above, the veil and the Absolute are not two different things: the veil is the external epiphany of the Absolute. From this point of view we must say that when man sees the veil, he is actually seeing nothing other than the very Absolute. In other words, the veil qua "veil" does cause obstruction to man's sight and prevents him from seeing the Absolute, but in its epiphanic form the veil is rather an immediate presentation of the Absolute itself. We must go a step further and say that the Absolute is so nakedly apparent to man's sight that it is not visible—another paradoxical situation in which light appears as darkness. As Shabastarí says: "The whole world of Being is the beams of the absolute Light. The Absolute remains hidden because it is so clearly manifest."[19]

Explicating this idea Láhíjí remarks: "Covering necessarily causes concealment, but it often happens also that the extremity of exposure causes concealment. Do you not see? In the middle of the day, when the sun is immediately exposed to view, the eye does not see the sun itself because of the excessive exposure of its light. In the same way, the Light of the existential Oneness,[20] because of its excessive exposure, remains invisible, being hidden in the very brilliancy of its own."[21]

"What a stupidity!" Shabastarí exclaims, "To search for the burning sun with the light of a candle, in the very midst of the desert!"[22] The burning sun does not conceal itself; it is there in the sky, fully exposed, fully in sight. There is no veil to obstruct the view. The phrase "in the very midst of the desert" suggests that the whole world of Being is a vast plain where there is absolutely no hindrance to the sight. Yet man is vainly searching for the sun with a candle in hand: the candle symbolizes human reason.

But the paradox of the veil has not yet reached its end. As we have already remarked, it is an empirical fact that the world of multiplicity is for the majority of men a veil concealing the metaphysical dimension of absolute unity. That is to say, as long as man considers the phenomenal things as self-subsistent and essentially existent entities, man can never hope to have an immediate vision of the Absolute which then conceals itself behind its own innumerable phenomenal forms. On the other hand, however—and here we observe another aspect of the paradox—it is precisely because of the actual existence of the veil that man can see the Absolute no matter how indirect, vague, and indistinct the vision may be. Of course he sees principally—And in most cases exclusively—multiplicity. But it may happen that he has a vague feeling that he is in the presence of something beyond. In such a case, it is through the veil of phenomenal things that he sees the light of the Absolute. Otherwise, the light is too strong to be seen. Says Shabastarí: "The eye has no power to stand the dazzling light of the sun. It can only see the sun as reflected in the water."[23]

Ontologically speaking, the water which, intervening between the eye and the sun, plays the role of a mirror, at the same time reducing the excessive radiancy of the sun, is the essential nonexistence of the things. It is only through the intermediary of this "mirror of non-existence" that existence becomes visible to our eyes. "Non-existence (*'adam*) is the mirror of absolute Existence (*hastí-ye mutlaq*), for it is in non-existence that the reflection of the radiancy of the Absolute becomes visible."[24]

It is to be remarked in this connection that in the metaphysical system of *wahdat al-wujúd*, or "unity of existence," the nonexistence which constitutes the essence of the phenomenal world begins to appear at a higher stage than that of the phenomenal world, namely at the stage of the "external archetypes" (*a'yán al-thábitah*). Rather, it is the non-existence of the eternal archetypes, properly speaking, that first reflects the pure light of the Absolute. What is observable at the stage of phenomenal things is nothing but an indirect, and therefore extremely weakened, reflection of this primary reflection.

The eternal archetypes, corresponding to what the philosophers call quiddities (*máhíyát*, sg. *máhíyah*) and resembling in many respects the Platonic Ideas, are in this school of thought conceived as the primary archetypal forms of things as they exist in the dimension of divine consciousness. As such they do exist in this particular dimension, but from the point of view of external, empirical existence they are non-existent, and remain forever nonexistent. And since it belongs to the very nature of nonexistence to stand opposed, in a certain sense, to existence, the eternal archetypes confront pure existence. The latter is reflected in this nonexistent mirror, or the nonexistent mirrors, and the existential light immediately appears diversified in accordance with the diversification of the mirrors.[25] The eternal archetypes are often called shadows; that is to say, they are essentially darkness and yet, in relation to the pure existence which they reflect, they are light. The appearance of the concrete things in the darkness of the phenomenal dimension is but a reflection of the pure light that has already been reflected in the dark mirror of the eternal archetypes.

VI

We shall now turn to a more subjective aspect of the problem and pursue the paradox of light and darkness in particular connection with the gradual development of the transcendental consciousness in the mystic who actually experiences the successive stages of the same paradox.

The whole process may briefly and in a provisional way be described as follows. When the Absolute (which is no other than pure light) appears in its uncontaminated unity to the consciousness of the mystic, all phenomenal distinctions disappear into darkness: no more consciousness of the perceiving subject; no more consciousness of the perceived objects. This is the mystic stage of *fanā'*, annihilation. The most salient paradoxical point at this stage is that by the full appearance of light in the consciousness all things disappear instead of appearing. Light in this respect is the cause of darkness. Yet, on the other hand, by the very fact that all things become deprived of their individual determinations and become obliterated from the consciousness—including this very consciousness from which they are obliterated—the whole world turns into a limitlessly vast ocean of light. And out of the depth of this ocean of light all the things that have once totally disappeared into darkness begin to emerge resuscitated and regain their individual determinations, being in themselves darkness but this time fully saturated with the pure light of existence. This is the mystic stage technically known as the stage of *baqá'*, survival in and with God.

The stage of *baqá'* is ontologically designated by the word *jam'* which literally means "gathering." Gathering is opposed to *farq* or "separating." This latter word refers to the ordinary empirical state in which the phenomenal things are separated and distinguished first from each other, and then from the Absolute. In this dimension man normally sees only the phenomenal world, and considers the Absolute—if man at all becomes aware of the existence of something beyond the phenomenal world—as the entirely "other" (*ghayr*).

In contrast to this, gathering, that is, unification, is the stage at which all the separate things are seen reduced to their original existential unity. All things, beginning with the self-consciousness of the mystic, disappear from awareness. The light of the phenomenal world is extinguished. There remains only absolute unity. There is not even the consciousness *of* the unity, for there is no trace here of any consciousness. The whole universe *is* unity. And the unity is light, but at the same time it is the darkness of the phenomenal world.

Out of the unfathomable abyss of this light-darkness, the mystic cries ou; "I am the Absolute!"[26] The reference is to the famous al-Halláj who, because of this and similar "blasphemous" utterances, was executed in 922 C.E. Concerning this particular utterance of al-Halláj, Láhíjí remarks:

> "He is one of the 'people of intoxication' (*arbáb-e sukr*) who in the state of inebriation disclose the divine secrets which are manifested to their purified minds. Since in that state

they have no ego-consciousness (*az bí-khudí*, literally "be-cause of without-self-ness") they cannot keep concealed whatever appears to them. Hence the 'I am the Absolute!' of al-Halláj. The utterance indicates that when the mystic traveling back to God through the way of self-purification goes beyond the region of multiplicity and becomes annihilated and absorbed into the ocean of unity, he discovers himself to be completely identical with the ocean of Reality of which he has been [in this ordinary consciousness] but a single drop. He is then a 'man of intoxication.' If he, in that state of inebriation suddenly cries out: 'I am the very Ocean itself!' because of his egolessness, we should not be surprised."[27]

VII

It is remarkable that in the process of the development of mystic consciousness light and darkness succeed one another, light itself being transformed into darkness and darkness itself being transformed into light. This process of interchange between light and darkness reaches the most crucial point with the appearance of an extraordinary state known as Black Light (*núr-e siyáh*). Black Light is a very delicate spiritual state into which the mystic enters just before *faná'* (annihilation) turns into *baqá'* (survival). It may be represented as a point which marks the end of *faná'* and the beginning of *baqá'*: it is the state shared by both.

As the mystic goes up the way of ascent toward the Absolute-as-such, he finally reaches a point at which he experiences his inner light, that is, his inner spiritual illumination, all of a sudden turning black. As actually experienced by the mystic, it is an epistemological darkness which is of a different nature from the ontological darkness that has been analyzed the foregoing, although, as we shall see presently, there is also an ontological aspect to it.

This epistemological darkness is a darkness caused by the extreme nearness of the mystic to the Absolute. Says Shabastarí: "An object of sight, when it approaches the eye too closely, darkens the sight, making the eye unable to see anything."[28] This is true, he comments, not only of the physical eye, but also of the "inner eye" (díde-ye bátin).

> "As the mystic in his ascent toward God goes beyond all the stages of the light of divine self-manifestation through His names and attributes [i.e., in the forms of the "eternal archetypes"], and becomes finally well prepared to receive His essential self-manifestation [i.e., God's revealing Himself directly, without any intermediary forms], suddenly the Light of this latter kind of self-manifestation appears to him in the color of utter blackness. Because of his extreme spiritual propinquity to God, the inner eye of the mystic turns dark and becomes powerless to see anything whatsoever."[29]

The mystic, as we have remarked earlier, is now at a stage just preceding the one in which the whole universe will transform itself into a limitless ocean of light. Rather, the darkness which he is now experiencing is *itself* the supreme light. "This blackness [siyáhí] in reality is the very light of the Absolute-as-such. In the midst of this darkness there is hidden the water of life."[30] The "water of life" means the state of baqá', the survival in God, the eternal life of existence.

Láhíjí recounts his own experience of black light:

> "Once, I found myself in a luminous, non-material world. The mountains and deserts were all in various colors of light, red, yellow, white, and azure. The luminous colors were lit-

erally fascinating. Under the overwhelming power of this extraordinary experience I was out of myself, I had lost my own self. All of a sudden I saw the whole universe being enveloped in black light. The sky, the earth, the air, every-thing turned into the same black light. I became totally annihilated in this black light, and remained consciousless. After a while, I came back to myself."[31]

What is subjectively experienced as black light corresponds to what is known objectively—that is, ontologically—as the stage of "oneness" (ahadíyah), to which reference has earlier been made.[32] It is also called "supreme blackness" (sawád-e a'zam). The oneness is the ontological stage of the Absolute-as-such prior to its manifesting itself in accordance with its inner articulations. Seen from the side of the phenomenal world, it is the supreme ontological dimension in which all empirical distinctions among things become annihilated and in which all things are absorbed into their original unity, or even beyond unity into the metaphysical nothingness which, paradoxically enough, is no other than the real plenitude of existence. In its aspect of nothingness this stage is experienced by the mystic as faná', while in its aspect of existential pleni-tude it is experienced as baqá'.

"The mystic," Láhíjí observes, "does not realize absolute existence (hastí-ye mutlaq) unless and until he fully realized absolute nothingness (nísti-ye mutlaq). Nothingness is in itself the very existence-by-the-Absolute. Absolute nothingness is revealed only in absolute existence . . . and absolute existence cannot be revealed except in the very midst of absolute Noth-ingness."[33] In short, nothingness (or darkness) is in reality existence (light), and light is in reality darkness.

VIII

Let us begin by reformulating in ontological terms what has just been described in the preceding section so that we might be better prepared to understand the nature of the paradox of light and darkness at its ultimate and highest stage.

The first thing to notice is that everything we perceive in the empirical world has without exception two different ontological aspects: the aspect of absolute reality (*haqíqah*), and the aspect of individuation (*tashakhkhus*) or determination (*ta 'ayyun*).

In the first aspect, everything is a self-manifestation (*tajallí*) of the Absolute; it is the appearance of the Absolute, not "as such," to be sure, but in a special form peculiar to the locus. It is an epiphany. In this sense everything is God.

In the second aspect, on the contrary, the same thing is considered in terms of its being something independent and self-subsistent. It is something "other" than the Absolute; it is non-God. From this point of view it is called a "creature" (*khalq*) and, philosophically, a "possible" (*mumkin*).[34] The important point is that "individuation" and "determination"—consequently the thing's being being independent and self-subsistent—are in truth fictitious (*i'tibárí*) properties that have no fundamental reality of their own and have been imposed upon the thing by the human mind.

Such being the case, the true knowledge of things will be gained, according to Shabastarí and Láhíjí, only when man (1) leaves the domain of multiplicity (which is in itself non-reality and non-thing), (2) betakes himself to the domain of unity (which is Reality-in-itself), and then (3) comes back again to the domain of multiplicity and witnesses in every individual thing of this domain the unity (which is the All) as it manifests itself there in its own self-determination. It goes without saying that the second stage in this process refers to the experience of *faná'* and the third to *baqá'*. Says Shabastarí: "[Real] thinking consists in proceeding from non-reality (*bátil*) toward Reality (*haqq*). It is to see the absolute All in every individual thing."[35] Note that Shabastarí here gives a definition of "thinking" (*tafakkur*) as it is understood by the theosophers, which is of a totally different nature from its ordinary definition. What is meant by "thinking" is *kashf*, "unveiling," that is, an immediate intuitive grasp of Reality, as opposed to *istidlál*, the process of reasoning by which one tries to arrive, on the basis of something known, at something unknown. The first half of Shabastarí's definition is a reference to *faná'*, which consists, as Láhíjí says, in "all the atoms in the world being effaced and annihilated in the beams of the Light of the divine unity, as drops of water in the sea."[36] The second half refers to *baqá'*, in which all the atoms, after having been absorbed into the ocean of unity—that is, after having been brought back to their original nothingness (*'adam-e aslí*)—are again revived as so many epiphanies of one single Reality.[37]

Thus the paradox of light and darkness reaches its culminating point, indicated by the peculiar expression: "bright night amidst the dark daylight" (*shab-e rowshan miyán-e rúz-e tárík*).[38] The structure of what is meant by this paradoxical expression is clarified by Láhíjí as follows:

> The *bright night* refers to the ontological stage of Oneness [*ahadíyah*] which is compared to *night* in respect of its being colorless and its absolute non-determination. For, just as in deep night nothing can be perceived, so in the region of the Divine Essence—which is the region where all phenomenal forms are annihilated—there can be no perception, no con-

sciousness. This is due to the fact that the Absolute-as-such, considered in its purity without any reference to possible relations, is not perceivable. Remember that at this stage every possible relation, every possible determination has been completely effaced.

But this *night* is said to be *bright* on the basis of the fact that in reality [i.e., apart from all consideration of the basic constitution of human cognition] the Absolute is by itself fully manifest and that all things are made apparent by the illumination of its Light.

Amidst the dark daylight refers to the fact that this absolute unity is manifested in the very midst of multiplicity, i.e. in all the phenomenal determinations which are, on the one hand, as clearly apparent as daylight and, on the other, as dark as night because of their essential non-reality and Darkness. multiplicity is apparent, yet at the same time it remains forever hidden.[39]

Láhíjí repeatedly states that the stage of *baqá'* is the ultimate stage to which the mystic can attain, and that it is the end of the spiritual journey, there being no further stage beyond it. But sometimes he seems to suggest the existence of a still higher stage which he designates as *faná' ba'da al-baqá'*, that is, the stage of "annihilation after survival."[40] It would be regarded as the second annihilation. In any case what is described by Láhíjí as the structure of this stage exactly corresponds to what Hua Yen Buddhism in China establishes as the ultimate of all ultimate ontological stages, the celebrated *ji-ji-muge-hokkai*, the "ontological dimension of unobstructed mutual interpenetration of all things." It also represents the extreme limit which our paradox of light and darkness can reach.

We have already seen that in the world view of the *wahdat*

al-wujúd school all things in the empirical world, even the single atoms of each thing, are each a particular form in which the Absolute manifests itself. Everything is a self-determination of the Absolute. In the terminology of Islamic theology this situation is often described by saying that everything is God as He is manifested in accordance with the essential requirement of a divine name. All divine names are ontologically the inner archetypal articulations of absolute Existence.

Thus everything in this world reflects in itself, in its own peculiar way, the Absolute. Everything is a mirror in which is reflected the Absolute. On the other hand, however, all things (that are in themselves darkness) are found to be one if they are traced back to the stage of absolute Oneness (which is light). From this point of view, each one of the things is the same as all others; it *is* the All. Thus when one thing reflects the Absolute in the form of one particular name, it is by that very act reflecting the Absolute in all names. This implies that in one single thing the Absolute is reflected in thousands of forms.

Says Shabastarí: "Behond, the whole world is a mirror, each one of the things is a mirror. Even in a single atom hundreds of suns are shining."[41] Again, "From one drop of water, if split apart, will hundreds of pure oceans gush forth."[42]

Láhíjí explicates this point in the following way:

> It has been established that every single divine name is in reality qualified by the properties of all other names, because all the Names are one at the stage of absolute oneness. The Names are differentiated from each other only by virtue of the secondary particularities of the attributes and relations. Thus it comes about that every single thing contains in itself all things. In one single grain of mustard-seed there are contained in reality [i.e., if observed apart from its individual

determination] all the things that exist in the world. It is only
because of its determination that all these things that are
contained therein do not come up to the surface. Thus the
mystic sees all things in everything. This is what is called the
"mystery of Divine self-manifestations" (*sirrr-e tajallíyát*).[43]

Here we are in the presence of the splendor of the paradox of light and darkness. The paradox weaves out a
magnificent tapestry in which numberless lights and
darknesses intersect each other and interpenetrate in such a
way that the whole universe is presented as a multidimensional and intricately shaded Temple of Light.

IX

We shall conclude by discussing, in terms of the paradox of
light and darkness, the position in the cosmos occupied by
man. This will make an apt conclusion because man is the
very embodiment of this cosmic paradox. Man in fact is represented in the metaphysical system of Shabastarí-Láhíjí as the
"intermediary stage (*barzakh*) between light and darkness."[44]
Moreover, the very paradox of light and darkness is actualized
only through the consciousness of man. In this sense man is
the center of the cosmic paradox.

As we have often observed, the phenomenal world is the
world of multiplicity, and as such it is a domain of darkness.
Man, who is a microcosmos (*'álam-e saghír*) in the sense that
all the prehuman ontological stages are realized in him, is the
extremity of multiplicity. That is to say, man is the ultimate
limit of darkness.

At the same time, however, man is an individual (*shakhs*)
in the real sense of the word. He is "one" just as the Absolute
is One. Thus in this particular respect there is a certain struc-

THE PARADOX OF LIGHT AND DARKNESS

tural similarity observable between the Absolute and man. For the Absolute is One in its essence, many in its attributes; man is also one in his personal individuality while being many in his properties, actions, and functions. This fact—that man comprises in himself "unity" and "multiplicity"—enables him to intuit through his own structure the cosmic paradox of unity qua unity being multiplicity and multiplicity qua multiplicity being unity.

"The very first thing that man realized," Láhíjí says, "is his own personal determination which is both the last of all the ontological stages in the 'descending arc' of the circle of existence, and the very first of all the stages in the 'ascending arc' of the same circle. Thus the ontological stage of man is called the 'appearance of the first light of the dawn' (*matla' al-fajr*), because man represents the end of the darkness of night (*niháyat-e zulmat-e shab*) and the beginning of the light of the day of unity (*bidáyat-e núr-e rúz-e wahdat*)."[45] Man is, in short, the *barzakh* between light and darkness. The whole cosmic drama of light and darkness is enacted in his mind.

NOTES

1. Muhammad Gíláni Láhíjí, *Mafátíh al-I'jáz fí Sharh-e Gulshan-e Ráz*, Kayván Samí'í, ed. (Tehran, 1956).

2. Henry Corbin, for instance, describes it as "une véritable somme de soufisme en persan." See his "Symboles choisis de la roseraie du mystere," *Trilogie Ismaélienne* (Téhéran and Paris, 1961), vol. 3, 28.

3. Aristotle, *Poetics* (trans. Bywater). 1957–1958.

4. Cf. Paul Henle, ed., "Metaphor," *Language, Thought, and Culture* (Ann Arbor, Mich., 1965), chap. 7.

5. Ibid., 175.

6. Shiháb al-Dín Yahyà al-Suhrawardí (1153–1191), one of the greatest mystic-philosophers of Persia, was known for his philosophy of light. Cf. Seyyed Hossein Nasr, "Suhrawardi and the Illuminationists," in *Three Muslim Sages* (Cambridge, Mass., 1964), 52–82.

7. The structure of the *faná'* and *baqá'* will be explained in detail later on in connection with the problem of the paradoxical relation between light and darkness. Also see chapter 1 for a further discussion of these states of the mystic.

8. *Hastí* is a Persian word of corresponding to the Arabic *wujud*; both mean exactly the same thing: "existence."

9. Láhíjí, 104.

10. Ibid., 98.

11. *Gulshan-e Ráz*, v. 126. The original word for "phenomenal thing" here is *mumkin*, i.e., "possible." The numbering of the verses throughout this paper is based on the text of *Gulsham-e Ráz* as it is reproduced in the Tehran edition of Láhíjí's commentary (cf. fn. 1).

12. Láhíjí, 72.

13. *Gulshan-e Ráz*, v. 115.

14. Láhíjí, 72, 89.

15. Ibid., 110.

18. Láhíjí, 99.

19. *Gulshan-e Ráz*, v. 97.

20. *Ahadíyah*, "absolute oneness," as distinguished from *wáhidíyah*, "oneness" (meaning the comprehensive "unity" of all things), constitutes in the metaphysical system of Láhíjí the highest stage of the Absolute qua existence.

21. Láhíjí, 72.

22. *Gulshan-e Ráz*, v. 94.

23. Ibid., v. 131.

24. Ibid., v. 133.

25. Cf. Láhíjí, 104–106.

26. *Gulshan-e Ráz*, v. 25: "Out of the ocean of unity a mystic cried out: I am the Absolute!" (*aná'l-haqq*)

27. Láhíjí, 29.
28. *Gulshan-e Ráz,* v. 122.
29. Láhíjí, 95.
30. *Gulshan-e Ráz,* v. 123.
31. Láhíjí, 96.
32. Cf. fn. 30.
33. Láhíjí, 100, 102–103.
34. Ibid., 9.
35. *Gulshan-e Ráz,* v. 72.
36. Láhíjí, 50.
37. Ibid., 51.
38. *Gulshan-e Ráz,* v. 128.
39. Láhíjí, 101.
40. Ibid., 115.
41. *Gulshan-e Ráz,* v. 145.
42. Ibid., v. 146.
43. Láhíjí, 115.
44. Ibid., 10.
45. Ibid.

CHAPTER 3

AN ANALYSIS OF WAHDAT AL-WUJÚD: TOWARD A METAPHILOSOPHY OF ORIENTAL PHILOSOPHIES

WAHDAT AL-WUJÚD, which may be translated as "oneness of existence" or "unity of existence" is a metaphysical concept going back to an outstanding Spanish Arab mystic-philosopher, Ibn 'Arabí, of the twelfth and thirteenth centuries (1165-1240 C.E.). But what I am concerned with, at least in this chapter, is the philosophical elaboration and development which this concept underwent in Iran in the periods subsequent to the Mongol invasion down to the sixteenth and seventeenth centuries when Sadr al-Din Shírází, or as he is more commonly called Mullá Sadrá (1571-1610 C.E.), achieved a grand synthesis of Iranian-Islamic philosophy precisely on the basis of this concept.

I am interested in this particular aspect of this particular problem out of all the interesting problems offered by the history of Iranian Islam, not necessarily because of my own personal philosophical attitude, but rather, and primarily, because of my conviction that the concept of *wahdat al-wujūd* is something which, if structurally analyzed and elaborated in a proper way, will provide a theoretical framework in terms of which we shall he able to clarify one of the most fundamental modes of thinking which characterize Oriental philosophy in general—not only Islamic philosophy, but most of the major historical forms of Oriental thought so that we might make a positive contribution from the standpoint of the philosophical minds of the East towards the much desired development of a new world philosophy based on the spiritual and intellectual heritages of East and West.

Living as we are in a critical moment of human history, we naturally feel urgent need for many things. One of these things is a better mutual understanding among various nations of the world, which is often talked about also as the task of promoting a better understanding between East and West. Mutual understanding between East and West is conceivable at a number of different levels. Here I am interested in only one of them; namely, the philosophical level of thinking.

It is undeniable that in the past attempts have sometimes been made to actualize a better mutual understanding between East and West at the level of philosophical thinking under the name of comparative philosophy. But it is no less undeniable that up until now comparative philosophy has remained rather in the peripheral regions of the intellectual activity of the philosophers. In most cases, the choice of the terms of comparison, to begin with, has been arbitrary, and the work consequently unsystematic. In short, comparative philosophy has, in my opinion, not been very successful, and it has not been given the kind of serious attention it duly deserves. And the main cause of this failure, I think, lies in its poverty in methodology.

In order to bring home the true significance of comparative philosophy, particularly for the purpose of promoting a real, deep philosophical understanding between East and West, it must first be developed in a more systematic way into what we might call a metaphilosophy of philosophies. I understand by metaphilosophy a comprehensive structural framework with a number of sub-structures at different levels, each of which will consist of a more or less large network of philosophical concepts that have analytically been taken out or worked out from the basic concepts found in the major philosophical traditions, both of East and West. The first practical step to be taken in the process of arriving at a metaphilosophy of this I nature will, at least in my case, consist in a careful semantic analysis of the structure of the key-concepts of each philosophical system. And the result will hopefully be a vast, very complicated, but well-organized and flexible conceptual system in which each individual system will he given its proper place and in terms of which the differences as well as the common grounds between the major philosophical schools of the East and West will systematically be clarified.

It is with such an ultimate aim in view that I am actually engaged in analyzing the key concepts of Oriental philosophies.[1] In this wide perspective, the concept of *wahdat al-wujūd* represents but a narrowly limited partial field. But it is of such a nature that, if we succeed in bringing to light its fundamental structure, it will provide a basic conceptual model by means of which the majority of Oriental philosophies will he brought up to a certain level of structural uniformity concerning at least one of their most fundamental aspects.

This attitude of mine would naturally imply that I am not considering the unity of existence as something exclusively Islamic or Iranian. Rather, I am interested here in this concept, and the philosophical possibilities it contains, as something representative of a basic structure which is commonly shared by many of the Oriental philosophies going back to divergent historical origins, like Vedantism, Buddhism, Taoism, and Confucianism. The structure of the philosophy of *wahdat al-wujūd* would in this perspective be seen to represent one typical pattern—an archetypal form, we might say—of philosophical thinking which one finds developed variously in more or less different forms by outstanding thinkers belonging to different cultural traditions in the East.

In undertaking a structural analysis of *wahdat al-wujūd*, I must emphasize at the very outset that I do not agree with those who tend to understand the word "structure" in a purely formal sense. For a structure understood in the sense of a mere form or a formal external system is almost of no value for the purpose of constructing the kind of metaphilosophy I am aiming at. Of course, I also take the word "structure" to mean a form or system. For my particular purpose, "structure" means a system with inner articulations, or to express the idea in more concrete terms, it is to be understood as a linguistic or conceptual system of higher order constituted by a number of more or less well-organized and well coordinated key philosophical concepts. The important point, however, is that the system must be grasped as an external form of an inner spirit or an original philosophical vision which lies behind it and which manifests itself in that particular form. Methodologically, the essential thing for us is first to grasp that central vision of a whole system or the spirit that animates the system from within and informs it, and then to describe the system as an organic evolvement of that central vision.

Approaching now *wahdat al-wujūd* from such a point of view, we find a magnificent system of metaphysics built up upon the basis of a peculiar vision of reality. As the very term *wahdat al-wujúd* or oneness of existence clearly indicates, this basic vision centers around "existence." In other words, the philosophy of *wahdat al-wujúd* is nothing other than a theoretical or rational reconstruction of an original metaphysical vision, which is conceived of as an intuition of the reality of existence (*wujúd*).

Having said this, I must immediately bring to your attention a very important fact; namely, that existence in this particular context is not the kind of existence of which all of us naturally have a common sense notion. Otherwise expressed, it is not existence as it is reflected in our ordinary, empirical consciousness. Rather it is existence as it reveals itself only to a transcendental consciousness. It is existence as intuited by man when he transcends the empirical dimension of cognition into the trans-empirical dimension of awareness.

We may recall at this juncture that the problem of existence was from the very beginning of the history of Islamic philosophy *the* metaphysical problem that Islam inherited from the tradition of Greek philosophy. It is important to remember, however, that in the earlier periods of Islamic philosophy, represented by such names as al-Kindí, al-Fárábí, Ibn Síná, and Ibn Rushd, *wujúd* or "existence," in the sense of the *act* of existing, was an object of philosophical concern only indirectly and, let us say, accidentally, in the sense that, following the age-old Aristotelian tradition of metaphysics, the primary concern of the thinkers was with *mawjúd* rather than *wujúd,* that is to say, "existent" or a concrete thing that exists rather than the act itself of existing. The problem of *wujúd* was raised and discussed mainly as part of the inner constitution of "existents," i.e. real things that exist.

It is highly significant that the primary emphasis was shifted from *existent* to *existence* in a drastic way only after Islamic philosophy passed through the furnace of profound mystical experience in the person of Ibn 'Arabi. Ibn Sīná in this respect stands just at the turning point, although as a matter of fact he still remains within the orbit of Aristotelian philosophy for in ontology he is concerned with the problem of *wujúd* (*actus essendi*) mainly as a constituent factor of *mawjúd* (*ens*). But at least we might safely say that he gave a decisive impetus to the later philosophical elaboration of the concept of *wahdat al-wujúd* by his explicit statement that existence is an accident or attribute of *máhíyah* or "quiddity." To this statement, however, he added another statement, namely that the accident called existence is not an ordinary accident, but that it is a very peculiar kind of accident. This is indeed an extremely important point which we must clarify as an indispensable preliminary to an analysis of *wahdat al-wujúd.*

At the empirical level of experience we constantly find ourselves surrounded by an infinite number of things, that is, substances that are qualified by various attributes or accidents. We distinguish a thing from its attributes by giving to the former an ontological status different from that of the latter. For at the level of daily, empirical experience, we naturally tend to think that the existence of the thing essentially precedes the existence of its attributes. That is to say, the attributes depend for their existence upon the thing, while the thing does not depend for its existence upon its attributes. We say for example: "The flower is white." It seems evident that the attribute "white" is actualizable only when the thing, the flower, is already existent, while the existence of the flower itself is not affected at all even if the flower loses its whiteness and changes its color.

This observation, however, does not apply to existence itself as an attribute. When for example we say: "The flower is existent," the actualization of the attribute does not presuppose the prior actualization of the flower. Quite the contrary, it is in this particular case the attribute that brings the flower into existence. This is in brief what Ibn Síná emphasized as a very peculiar nature of "existence" as an accident. It is an "accident," he says, but it is not an ordinary accident; it behaves in a totally different way from all other accidents.

Now in the view of those who belong to the school of *wahdat al-wujúd,* this extraordinary or exceptional nature of existence as an accident comes from the very simple fact that in reality existence is not an accident of anything at all. But the problem arises precisely because existence, which in reality is not an accident, is grammatically and logically treated as an accident and is made to function as a predicate. Thus we say: "The flower is existent" just in the same way as we say: "The flower is white," as if these two propositions stood semantically quite on a par with each other.

But according to the people of *wahdat al-wujúd,* there is in truth a fundamental difference between the two types of propositions with regard to their semantic behavior, i.e., with regard to the external structure of reality to which each one of them refers. In the case of propositions of the type: "The flower is white," there is a structural correspondence between grammar and external reality. Otherwise expressed, the grammatical or logical form of the sentence imitates and reproduces the structure of the external reality to which the proposition is intended to refer. But in existential propositions of the type: "The flower is existent," there is a glaring discrepancy between the grammatical form and external reality. Grammatically or logically, the "flower" is the subject, and as such it denotes a self-subsistent substance, while the predicate "existent" denotes a quality which qualifies and determines in a certain way the substance. But in the view of the people of *wahdat al-wujúd*, the flower in reality is not the subject; the real ultimate subject is "existence," while the flower, or for that matter any other so-called things, are but qualities or attributes variously determining the eternal, ultimate subject which is "existence." Grammatically, "flower" for example is a noun, but metaphysically it is an adjective. All so-called things are adjectives or adjectival in nature, modifying and qualifying the sole reality called "existence."

As one can easily see, this position exactly corresponds to the position taken by Advaita Vedanta regarding the same problem. In Vedanta, too, the Absolute which is indicated by the word *Brahman* is conceived as pure being or existence (*Sat*) all pervasive, non-temporal, non-spatial, absolutely unqualified and unlimited—while all so-called "things" are considered so many determinations and particularizations of this absolute Indeterminate. That is to say, here too, all quiddities are adjectival to "existence."

Thus the structure of external reality which is indicated by the proposition: "The flower is existent" proves to be completely different from what is suggested by the grammatical form of the sentence. What is existent in the fullest sense of the word is existence as the absolute Indeterminate, not the flower. Being-a-flower is but a special self-determination of this absolute Indeterminate. It is but a particular phenomenal form in which existence reveals itself in the dimension of the so-called external, sensible world. In other words, the "flower" here is an accident qualifying "existence," and determining it into a certain phenomenal form. Existence in itself, that is, in its purity, is without attributes. It is an absolutely simple unity or an absolute indiscrimination. Consequently, all differences that are perceivable at the level of sensible experience among various things are to be judged illusory. It is in this sense that Advaita Vedanta represented by Shankara declares: that all phenomenal things are nothing but illusions, that they are all illusory forms "super-imposed" (adhyása) upon the underlying pure unity of Brahman.

Both Taoism and Mahayana Buddhism take exactly the same position with regard to the nature of the seemingly self-subsistent things of the sensible world. Both are characterized by a thoroughgoing anti-essentialism. They are definitely against the position which in the Islamic tradition of meta-physics is known as the thesis of asálat al-máhíyah, i.e. the thesis that the various quiddities which we observe in the external world are possessed of a fundamental reality. Thus to give an example, the author of the Ta Ch'éng Ch'i Hsin Lun ("The Awakening of Faith in Mahayana") which is regarded as one of the most basic philosophical textbooks of Mahayana Buddhism, remarks: "All men who are not yet enlightened discriminate with their deluded minds from moment to moment between things (i.e. differentiate the original absolute unity of Reality into various self-subsistent things), and become thereby estranged from the absolute Reality." The phenomenal things thus established by the discriminating activity of the mind are very significantly called jan fa "things of defilement," that is to say, the phenomenal things are here ontologically regarded as elements that "defile" and deform the purity of the one Reality. Again, in the same book we find the following very straightforward statement of this position: "That which is known as the Mind-Nature (i.e. absolute Reality) is beyond all phenomenal determinations. It is only through illusions that all things become distinguished from one another as independent entities. Once we are freed from the illusion-producing movements of our minds, there will no longer be any appearance of the so-called objective world."

But this statement, namely, that the things of the phenomenal world are all illusory appearances, requires partial correction, for the superimpositions that have just been mentioned are considered in Vedantism, Buddhism and Islam alike, to be caused not only by the relative, and intrinsically limited epistemological structure of the human mind but also by the very structure of absolute Reality itself. I shall come back presently to this important point.

It would seem that the brief explanation I have just given of the basic standpoint of *wahdat al-wujúd* type of philosophy has made us realize that we are in the presence of two metaphysical views of Reality which stand in sharp opposition to each other, an opposition which we may designate in a provisional way as "essentialism" versus "existentialism."

The first, essentialism, is a philosophical elaboration or extension of our ordinary common sense view of things. In fact, at the level of our daily encounter with the world, we observe everywhere around us "things," i.e. quiddities or essences that are existent. In this perspective it is the quiddities that exist. Everything that we observe here is "something that exists," i.e. *mawjúd* or *ens.* Nowhere is existence (*wujúd*) itself as pure *actus essendi* observable in its immediate, pure state. It is always hidden behind the innumerable quiddities. In this view, it is the quiddities that exist, while existence is but an attribute or property of the quiddities.

In what we propose to designate by the word "existentialism," on the contrary, we find this relationship between quiddity and existence completely reversed. Existence is here the basis; it is in fact the sole Reality, and the quiddities are found to be adjectival to it; they are to be considered attributes qualifying the unique Reality.

It is important to remark that "essentialism" and "existentialism" as understood in this particular context do not stand opposed to each other on one single level of human experience. For unlike "essentialism" which, as I have said above, is a natural philosophical development of the ordinary ontological experiences shared by all persons, "existentialism" in this context means a transcendental existentialism in the sense that it is a metaphysical system based upon, and born out of an ecstatic, mystical intuition of Reality as it discloses itself to a transcendental consciousness in the depths of concentrated meditation.

It will be interesting to observe in this connection that the Buddhist term for the Absolute is in Sanskrit *tathatá* whose Chinese translation is *chén ju* (which is read in Japanese *shinnyo*). *Tathatá* literally means "suchness," and *chén ju* "truly-such." That is to say, in both cases, the Absolute is referred to by words that signify "being as it really is or existence as it naturally is." But the expression "existence as it naturally is" does not refer to existence of things as we know it at the empirical level of experience. "Existence" here means the reality of existence as it reveals itself to us when we are in the state of contemplation, through the activation of the transcendental function of our mind, that is to say, the reality of existence prior to its being "defiled" and deformed by the discriminating activity of the ordinary consciousness in its waking experience. In Islam, this activation of the transcendental function of the mind is designated by a number of technical terms, the most important of them being the word *kashf*, which literally means "unveiling" or "taking off the veil." And the inner structure of this experience is usually described in terms of *fanā'* and *baqā'*.[2]

Here I shall confine myself to considering very briefly the theoretical aspect of the problem regarding how this kind of experience provides a basis upon which one could build up the metaphysical system of *wahdat al-wujūd*.

The first of the two words, *fanā'*, literally means "extinction" or something being annihilated, somewhat like the Buddhist concept of *nirvāna*. In the particular context in which we are interested, it means the total annihilation of an individual's ego-consciousness resulting from an intense concentration of the mind in deep meditation. In this experience, the seemingly hard crust of the empirical consciousness of the mystic is dissolved and the ego-substance becomes totally absorbed into the underlying unity of existence.

The metaphysical significance of this subjective annihilation lies in the fact that existence that has up to that moment been appearing in the pseudo-substantial form of an ego, loses this determination and turns back to its own original absolute indetermination. And since the human mind is the only locus in which anything can be subjectively actualized, existence too, becomes actualized or realized in its pure subjectivity only through man's experiencing the total dissolution of his own pseudo-subjectivity. This is what is referred to in Vedanta as man's realizing the total identification of *Átman* with *Brahman*.

We must recall at this point that the metaphysical Reality in its purity is the absolute Indeterminate, and as such it defies all objectification, for objectification implies determination. The moment existence is grasped as an object, it ceases to be itself. existence in its original indetermination can never be taken hold of as an object. It can only be realized as the subject of all knowledge in the form of man's self-realization, for it is the ultimate Subject. This is—be it remarked in passing—why existence in its absolute indetermination is in Buddhism often called the Mind-Nature or Mind-Reality.

As the narrowly limited ego-consciousness of man thus becomes dissolved and absorbed into the limitless expanse of the absolute Consciousness, and as existence that has been crystallized into the determined form of an ego-substance returns to its original all-pervasive indetermination, all the determined forms of the objective world also go back to their original existential indetermination. For there is a fundamental functional correlation between the subjective state of the mind and the objective state of the external world. Where there is no subject, i.e. ego-substance to see things, there is no longer anything to be seen as an object. As a famous metaphor shared by so many Oriental thinkers goes: as all the waves that have been raging on the surface of the ocean calm down, the limitless Ocean alone remains visible in its eternal tranquility.

Metaphysically this is the stage of Nothingness for there is here neither subject nor object. But since the word "Nothingness" refers to existence in its pure and absolute indetermination, the stage is also called by another name which is of a more positive nature, namely, oneness or unity. The Buddhists often describe it as "one single piece with no articulation." The Taoist philosopher Chuang Tzu calls it "chaos" (*hun tun*). It is at this stage or from the viewpoint of this stage only that all the different things that are discernible in the empirical world are declared to be illusory. It is also from such a peculiar point of view that the Muslim philosopher, Mulla Sadrā, regards the so-called empirical things as "sheer connections" (*rawābit mahdah*) with no self-subsistence of their own. The representative Vedanta philosopher, Shankara, considers them as name-and-form (*nāma-rūpa*), multiplicity superimposed by ignorance (*avidyā*). At the next stage, however, this veil of illusoriness is again removed from the things of the empirical world. The next stage is the stage of *baqā'* experience.

Baqa' means "remaining" or "survival." Technically it refers to the spiritual stage at which all the things of the world that have once been dissolved into Nothingness and that have been lost in the absolute indiscriminate unity of "existence," become resuscitated out of the very depth of the Nothingness. The entire phenomenal world of multiplicity with its infinitely various and variegated forms again begins to evolve itself before man's eyes.

There is, however, a fundamental difference between the world of multiplicity as observed at this stage and the same empirical world of multiplicity as it appears to man before he passes through the stage of *fanā'*. For at the stage of *fanā'* man observes how all the things of the world lose their seeming ontological solidity, become fluid, and finally become lost into the original absolute indiscrimination of "existence." Now at the stage of *baqā'*, the same things are observed as they loom up out of the very Ground of that absolute indiscrimination and regain their reality in the dimension of waking experience.

Thus the things are again established as so many different things which are clearly distinguishable from each other. And yet they appear this time deprived of self-subsistence. They are there, but not as self-subsistent entities; rather they are there as so many particularizations and self-determinations of the absolute Indeterminate. In this respect they are not to be regarded as sheer illusions. For they *are* real in so far as each one of them is a particular form into which the Absolute has determined itself and in which the Absolute manifests itself. But they are empty and illusory if one considers them without reference to the original metaphysical Ground of which they are but various manifestations. They are illusory in so far as they are considered to be particular "things," self-subsistent and self-sufficient.

In reference to the ontological status of the phenomenal things, the Muslim thinkers of the *wahdat al-wujúd* school often use expressions like *wujúd i'tibárí*, i.e. "fictitious existence," and *wujúd majází*, i.e. "metaphorical or transferred existence." These and other similar expressions simply mean that the things of the empirical world are sheer nothing if considered in isolation from the underlying unity of existence, but that they are really existent if considered in relation to the latter. We have already seen above how Mulla Sadrá calls the things of the empirical world "sheer connections," that is, sheer relations. But the word "relation" (*idáfah*) should not be taken in the sense of an ordinary relation subsisting between two terms each of which is conceived as a self-subsistent entity. For in this particular context, "relation" means "illuminative relation" (*idáfah ishráqíyah*). That is to say, the things of the empirical world are established as partial realities only through the illuminative or self-manifesting act of the one absolute Reality.

This Islamic view is in perfect agreement with the position taken by Shankara regarding the problem of the reality and unreality of the empirical world. Like Muslim thinkers, Shankara takes the position that the empirical world is not ultimately and absolutely real, but that it is *relatively* real. It is not ultimately real because Brahman is not, and cannot be, experienced in the empirical world in its ultimate and absolute aspect, which is absolute indetermination. And yet, on the other hand, the empirical world is not entirely devoid of an objective basis of reality. Suppose, Shankara argues, a man sees a rope lying on the ground, and takes it for a snake. The snake that appears to the eyes of the man is illusory, because in reality it is nothing but a rope. But the snake is not sheer nothing either, in so far as it has its objective basis in a really existent rope. In a somewhat similar way, each one of the things which we see in the empirical world has an objective ontological basis in Brahman. For, according to Shankara, every single phase of our waking experience *is* a real experience of Brahman. In a famous passage in the *Viveka-Cúdámani* (521) he says: "The world is an unbroken series of Brahman perceptions, so that the world is in all respects no other than Brahman." That is to say, whenever we perceive something in this world we are in reality perceiving Brahman itself, not in its absolute aspect, to be sure, but in one of its particular phenomenal forms. In this sense, the empirical world is not an illusion; it is possessed of *vyávahárika*-reality, i.e. relative reality peculiar to the dimension of empirical experience, which it acquires in the capacity of a self-determination of Brahman, although from the absolute viewpoint, i.e. from the viewpoint of Brahman in its absolute purity, the empirical world is essentially illusory.

The theoretical basis that underlies this argument in the case of Shankara is the thesis known as *sat-kárya-váda*, i.e. the doctrine that the effect is but a relative and conditioned manifestation of the cause, there being between the two no real separation. The empirical world in this view is nothing other than Brahman-as-the-world.

Exactly the same explanation is applicable to the view taken by the philosophers of the *wahdat al-wujúd* school on the relationship between *haqq* and *khalq*, i.e. between absolute Reality and the created world. Thus to give one example, according to 'Abd al-Karím al-Jílí (1365-c.-1421 C.E.), the well-known author of the book *Al-insán al-kámil* ("The Perfect Man"), to call the things of this world "creatures" or "created things" is simply to call them by a "borrowed" name. Not that the various things and properties that are observable in this world are "borrowings." They are not "borrowings;" they are God Himself in the sense that they are various phenomenal forms assumed by the Absolute as it manifests itself at the level of the empirical experience of human perception. Only the name of "creatureliness" (*khalqíyah*) is a borrowing. God "lends" this name to His own attributes in so far as they appear in the empirical world. "Thus," Jílí says, "the Absolute (*haqq*) is, as it were, the prime matter of this world. The world in this sense is comparable to ice, and the Absolute to water which is the material basis of ice. The congealed mass of water is called 'ice,' which is but a borrowed name; its true name is 'water.'"

All this naturally leads the philosophers of the *wahdat al-wujúd* school to the conclusion that whatever is observable in this world has without exception two different aspects: (1) the divine aspect or the aspect in which it is absolute Reality itself, and (2) the creaturely aspect or the aspect in which it is something relative, something other than absolute Reality. One might describe this situation in plain language by saying: Everything in this world is in a certain sense God, and in another a creature. A creature *qua* creature is distinguishable, and must be distinguished, from God. But the creatureliness is ultimately reducible to divine Nature in so far as the former is an "illuminative relation" of the latter itself.

In order to explain the delicate relationship between these two aspects that are recognizable in everything, Muslim thinkers have proposed a number of metaphors. One of the most commonly mentioned is the metaphor of water and waves, which is also a favorite metaphor of the Mahayana Buddhists. I shall give here another typical one as explained by Haydar Ámulí, an outstanding Iranian philosopher of the fourteenth century, in his *Jami' al-Asrár*.[3] It is a metaphor based on a peculiar relationship between ink and the letters written with it. Ink structurally corresponds to the all-pervasive unique reality of existence while the letters written with it correspond to the quiddities *(máhíyát)* as actualized in the forms of the various things in the empirical world. Here follows the gist of what Haydar Ámulí says about this metaphor.[4]

Suppose we are reading a book. Our attention naturally is drawn toward the written letters. What strikes our eyes are primarily letters. We take notice only of the letters. We do not see the ink with which they are written. We are not even aware of the ink, while in reality we are seeing nothing other than various forms assumed by the ink. A slight shift of viewpoint will immediately make us realize that the letters are but of a "fictitious" *(i'tibárí)* nature. What really exists before our eyes is ink, nothing else. The seeming reality of letters is after all due to social convention. They are not realities *(haqá'iq)* in the most fundamental sense. Yet, on the other hand, it is equally undeniable that the letters do exist and are real in so far as they are various forms assumed by the ink which is the sole reality in this case.

Everything in this world is comparable to a letter in its double nature that has just been explained. Those who perceive only letters without taking notice of the underlying reality of ink are those whose eyes are veiled by the letters. To this fact refers the famous *hadith* which says: "God is concealed behind seventy thousand veils of light and darkness." Those who recognize only the veils and do not recognize the hidden God behind them are, theologically, outspoken and straightforward infidels. Those who know at least vaguely the existence of the invisible God behind and beyond the visible veils are believers and monotheists in an ordinary sense. But they are imperfect monotheists or imperfect "men of unification" (*muwahhidún*) because what they actually perceive is nothing but letters, while in reality the ink is so clearly and nakedly visible in the letters. Letters are not even veils, for they are the ink. It is in reference to this point that Ibn 'Arabi says: "It is the empirical world that is a mystery, something eternally hidden and concealed, while the Absolute is the eternally Apparent that has never concealed itself. The ordinary people are in this respect completely mistaken. They think that the world is the apparent and the Absolute is a hidden mystery."

But, Haydar Ámulí continues to say, those who see only and exclusively the ink without taking notice of the letters are also imperfect monotheists, for their eyes are veiled by the ink from the vision of the concrete forms assumed by the ink itself. A real "man of unification" must be a "man of two eyes" (*dhu 'aynayn*) whose vision is veiled by nothing—neither by ink nor by letters—a man, in other words, who sees unity in multiplicity and multiplicity in unity.

The metaphor of ink and letters together with what preceded it has, I believe, made it abundantly clear that according to the thinkers of the school of *wahdat al-wujúd,*' existence (*wujúd*) is something that is one single reality (*haqíqah*) and that has many divergent manifestation-forms (*mazáhir*). This position is established upon the fundamental vision of the act of "existence," which is the one absolute reality, running through, or flowing through, all things in the universe. This is what is called *sarayán al-wujúd,* i.e. the "pervasion of existence," or *inbisát al-wujúd,* i.e. the "unfolding of existence." This fundamental vision of the reality of existence running through the whole universe, or rather we should say, producing the whole world of Being as various forms of its self-unfolding, has led the thinkers of this school toward constructing a metaphysical system in which the same reality of existence is given a number of degrees or stages in accordance with the various degrees of its self-unfolding or self-manifestation.

In what follows I shall try to analyze the basic structure of this system in its most typical form. In so doing we shall have to confine our attention to the broad outlines of the problem which in reality is an extremely complicated one, particularly if we are to take into account the details of the historical development of the thought. There is in fact no perfect uniformity recognizable among the various systems that have been proposed by the representative thinkers of this school except with regard to the most fundamental metaphysical insight into the mystery of existence and with regard to the very general structural principles upon which they are constructed. Otherwise, there is no unanimity even with regard to the number of the major stages or degrees to be distinguished. The particular system which I am going to analyze here is an archetypal one in the sense that (1) its basic structure is more or less commonly shared by the majority of the systems, and that (2) it is formally of such a nature that it allows of the widest application in the broader perspective of metaphilosophical considerations.

One of the basic points on which all thinkers of the *wahdat al-wujúd* school are in perfect agreement with each other is that the Absolute itself has two aspects that are turned toward opposite directions: *bátin* and *záhir*, i.e. interior and exterior. The first of these, the *bátin* or interior, is the self-concealing aspect of the Absolute, while the second, the *záhir* or exterior, is its self-revealing aspect.

In its first aspect, the Absolute is an absolute unknown-unknowable. It is an eternal metaphysical mystery. Religiously, the Absolute here is the hidden God. Thus from the viewpoint of human cognition, it is the purely negative side of the Absolute, although from the viewpoint of the Absolute itself it is the most positive of all its possible aspects, for it is the unconditional plenitude of existence.

The second aspect, the *záhir* or exterior, on the contrary, represents for the human mind the positive aspect of the Absolute. In this aspect the Absolute is the metaphysical Source of the phenomenal world. Theologically the Absolute here is the self-revealing God. Through this aspect the Absolute manifests itself as various things at various stages which we are going to observe.

This basic distinction between the positive and negative aspects in the metaphysical constitution of the Absolute is common to all the major Oriental philosophies other than Islamic. In Vedanta, for instance, we have the celebrated thesis of *dvi-rúpa Brahma* "two-fold Brahman," that is, the distinction between the *nirguna Brahman* and *saguna Brahman*, i.e. the absolutely attributeless Brahman and the self-same Brahman adorned with all kinds of attributes. In Buddhism we have the distinction between "Suchness as absolute Nothingness" and "Suchness as non-Nothingness." Taoists distinguish between Non-Being and Being. Confucianists distinguish between *wu chi* (the Ultimateless) and *t'ai chi* (the Supreme Ultimate.)

It will be evident that, if we are to divide theoretically the entire sphere of existence into a certain number of metaphysical regions or stages, the Absolute in its *bátin* "interior" aspect will occupy the highest position. For the Absolute in its interior aspect *is* the Absolute itself pure and simple. Ontologically it is *dhat al-wujúd*, i.e. existence itself, or existence in its absolute purity. Theologically it is *dhat alláh*, i.e. the very Essence of God as God is supposed to be before being described by any attribute at all.

But it is noteworthy that already at this stage divergence of opinions begins to appear among the thinkers. According to quite a number of representative thinkers, existence-itself, i.e. existence at the highest stage, is existence in the state of an absolute transcendence. It is sheer metaphysical indiscrimination or the absolute Indeterminate to which reference was made in an earlier context. And since it infinitely transcends all relative distinctions, it is indescribable and ineffable. It is therefore essentially unknown and unknowable. It is a great Mystery (*ghayb*). The utmost we can say of this stage is that it is "one," not in the numerical sense but absolutely, in the sense that nothing is here visible, nothing is discernible. Technically this stage is known as the stage of *ahadíyah* or "absolute Oneness."

There are, however, some thinkers who do not remain satisfied with this view, and who insist on pushing the highest stage of existence further beyond *ahadíyah*.

Against those who see in *ahadíyah* the ultimate metaphysical stage—Dá'úd Qaysarí (d. 1350 C.E.) is one of them—they think that it is not completely right to equate the *ahadíyah* directly with "existence-itself" in its absolute purity. Certainly they admit that the *ahadíyah* is contained within the confines of the metaphysical region of the *dhat al-wujúd*, i.e. "existence-itself" in its purity, because it is sheer indiscrimination, the pure reality of existence without even an internal articulation, not to speak of external articulation. It is also absolute in the sense that it is absolute transcendence. But existence at this stage is *not* absolute in that it is determined at least by transcendence. It is conditioned at least by the condition of transcending all conditions. Those who think this way—'Abd al-Karím Jílí is one of them—take the position that the absolutely ultimate stage of existence must be beyond even the condition of unconditionality and transcendence. And since existence at this stage is unconditional to such an extent that it is not delimited even by being unconditional, it cannot but be absolute Nothingness from the point of view of human cognition. It is in this sense called the *ghayb al-ghuyúb*, the "Mystery of Mysteries," corresponding exactly to Lao Tzu's *hsüan chih yu hsüan*, which also can most appropriately be translated as "Mystery of Mysteries" or "Mystery beyond Mysteries." It was in order to give a logical formulation to this concept that the Taoist philosopher Chuang Tzu (fourth century B.C.E.) devised the formula *wu-wu-wu* or "Non-Non-Non-Being." Its last element, i.e. "Non-Being" is the simple negation of the empirical existence of phenomenal things. The second, i.e. Non-(Non-Being) is intended to be the absolute negation of the first, relative negation, and as such it refers to the total and unconditional indiscrimination of "existence," corresponding to the *ahadíyah*. The third, i.e. Non-{Non-(Non-Being)} negates this very unconditionality, thus corresponding to the Islamic concept of "Mystery of Mysteries."[5]

In the technical terminology of later Islamic metaphysics, the "Mystery of Mysteries" is called "existence as absolutely non-conditioned" (*lá bi-shart maqsamí*) in contrast to the stage of *ahadíyah* which is called "existence as negatively conditioned" (*bi-shart lá*). "Negatively conditioned" means that existence at this stage is conditioned at least by being not conditioned by any determination.

In this second system, namely, the system in which the "Mystery of Mysteries" is placed at the highest and ultimate position, the *ahadíyah* is naturally relegated to the second place. Unlike in the first system, the *ahadíyah* or the "absolute Oneness" is no longer considered to be the pure reality of existence prior to any self-determination. Quite the contrary, the *ahadíyah* here is the stage of the first self-determination (*ta'ayyun awwal*) of the Absolute. It is the second of the metaphysical stages of existence, and is naturally a step closer toward the world of created things. It is interesting in this respect that Lao Tzu who refers to the absolutely unconditional aspect of the Way (*tao*) as the Mystery of Mysteries, immediately turns to its positive aspect and describes the Way in that aspect as the "Gateway of myriad wonders,"[10] that is, the Gateway through which emerge all things into the phenomenal world. In the Islamic view too, the *ahadíyah* is the source of all phenomenal things.

In fact, it is from the very midst of the *ahadíyah* that the creative activity of the Absolute, i.e. the self-manifesting act of pure existence, arises. This self-manifesting act of existence is technically known as the "most sacred emanation" (*fayd aqdas*). The result of this emanation is the appearance of the next metaphysical stage, that of *wáhidíyah* or Unity.

Figure 1

At the stage of *wáhidíyah*, the reality of existence still maintains its original unity unimpaired, there being no external multiplicity manifested. Internally, however, the unity is here definitely articulated, although this is not yet the stage of the appearance of the phenomenal world. (Figure 1)

The real situation will become clear if we approach the matter from the reverse side, that is, from the viewpoint of the human consciousness which, starting from the phenomenal commotion of the things of the empirical world, is gradually elevated in deep meditation up to this stage. From this viewpoint, the *wáhidíyah* will appear

Figure 2

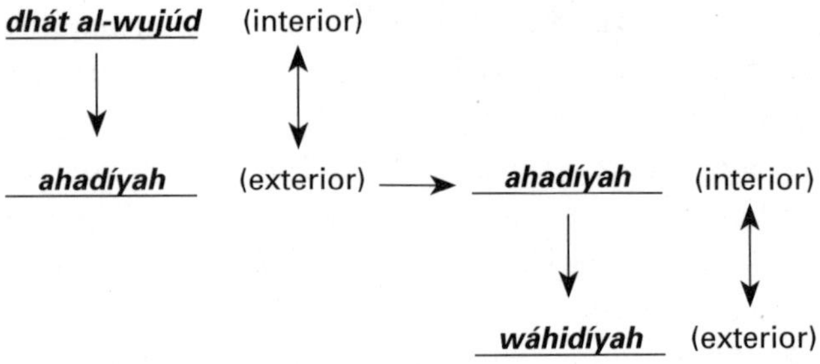

dhát al-wujúd (interior)

ahadíyah (exterior) ⟶ **_ahadíyah_** (interior)

wáhidíyah (exterior)

as the stage at which all the things, qualities, and events that have been raging with universal commotion in the phenomenal world become fused together into a vast unity. Thus, the *wáhidíyah* is not existential unity pure and simple as is the case with *ahadíyah*, but rather a comprehensive unity of an infinity of different things. The *wáhidíyah* in this sense is unity with inner articulations. But since, as we have just seen, the *wáhidíyah* is but the "exterior" of the *ahadíyah*, the inner articulations of the *wáhidíyah* must be considered to be the external appearance of the hidden articulations inherent in the *ahadíyah* itself. The *ahadíyah*, considered in itself is pure and absolute Oneness, there being not even a shadow of multiplicity. But if considered in relation to, and from the point of view of, the stage of *wáhidíyah*, it is found to contain in itself a principle of diversity. (Figure 2)

The principle of ontological diversity which plays an exceedingly important role in Vedanta under the name of *máyá* and in Mahayana Buddhism as *avidyá*, nescience or ignorance—the word ignorance here being understood in a cosmic sense—is in the philosophy of *wahdat al-wujúd* under-stood and described in terms of Love (*hubb*). This peculiar concept of Love is based on a celebrated *hadith qudsi* which reads: "I was a hidden treasure, and I loved to be known. Thus I created the creatures so that I might be known" (*kuntu kanzan makhfiyan, fa-ahbabtu an u'rafa, fa-khalqatu al-khalaqa li-hay u'rafa*).[6]

The phrase "hidden treasure" refers to the stage of *ahadíyah*, particularly in reference to the "exterior" aspect of the *ahadíyah*; namely, that aspect in which the *ahadíyah* is turned toward the phenomenal world.[7] For in this particular aspect, the ahadíyah is the ultimate source or Ground of all things that are to come out in concrete forms in the subsequent ontological dimensions, although in its interior aspect, i.e. that aspect in which it is turned toward the opposite direction, i.e. toward its own Source which is the "Mystery of Mysteries," the *ahadíyah* is nothing but pure Oneness.

Thus the *ahadíyah* considered in its "exterior" aspect is here designated as a "hidden treasure." The concept of "hidden treasure" is in its structure very close to Lao Tzu's concept of the "Gateway of myriad wonders" which, as has just been mentioned, indicates Tao or absolute Reality considered as the ultimate Source of all phenomenal things. Similarly the "hidden treasure" is rightly to be compared with the Buddhist concept of *tathágata-garbha*, the "Storehouse of the Absolute" which is also the absolute unity of existence in the particular aspect in which it is turned toward *samsára*, "birth and death," i.e. the world of phenomenal transiency. The Storehouse of the Absolute is still absolutely one and immovable, but it somehow contains in itself a moving drive which, once activated, pushes the Absolute towards phenomenal evolvement.

The same is true of the ontological function of love in the

Islamic system. The creative movement, or, to use the technical terminology of *wahdat al-wujūd* philosophy, the self-manifestation (*tajallī*) of the Absolute which is activated by the principle of love, emerges for the first time at the stage of *ahadíyah* and is called the "most sacred Emanation."[8] As the result of this Emanation, the stage of *wáhidíyah* becomes established. The *wáhidíyah*, is the ontological stage at which the original absolute Oneness of the reality of existence appears with inner articulations. These inner articulations are called, in accordance with the traditional terminology of theology, divine Names and Attributes. In this sense the stage of *wáhidíyah* is called the stage of the Names and Attributes (*asmá' wa-sifát*). Another name of this stage is the stage of knowledge (*'ilm*), i.e. divine Consciousness. This appellation comes from the idea that the *wáhidíyah* is the stage at which God becomes conscious of Himself in the form of His own essential Perfections (*kamálát dhátíyah*). The essential Perfections of God that are thus established in divine Consciousness with clear demarcations are called the "eternal Archetypes" (*a'yán thábitah*). Structurally, each eternal Archetype is considered to be the *záhir* or exterior of particular divine Name which is the *bátin* or interior of the Archetype. The eternal Archetypes are to be regarded as ontological models which are eternally established in divine Consciousness and upon which the phenomenal things are produced in the empirical dimension of time and space.

Ontologically, the stage of *wáhidíyah* is called *wujúd bi shart shay'*, i.e. existence-as-conditioned-by-being-something, which means existence as determined into the forms of particular things, not yet in the external world, to be sure, but in the eternal, supra-temporal, and supra-spatial dimension. Such a conception of the eternal archetypes clarifies the position taken by the philosophers of *wahdat al-wujúd* with regard to the notorious problem of universals. They necessarily hold the thesis of *universalia ante res,* for the eternal Archetypes are real because the inner articulations of the *wáhidíyah,* of which they are the external appearances, are definitely real. But in terms of the concrete empirical world, the Archetypes are not really existent. This is what is meant by Ibn 'Arabí when he says that "the eternal Archetypes have not yet smelled the fragrance of existence," the word existence in this context meaning empirical existence.

The eternal Archetypes become actualized as individual phenomenal things only at the next stage, that of the concrete existents, or the world of creaturely things. And the creative or self-manifesting activity of the absolute reality of existence by which this ontological "descent" is actualized is called the "sacred emanation" (*fayd muqaddas*) in distinction from the "most sacred emanation" by which the *ahadíyah* develops into *wáhidíyah.*

Thus we have come down from the height of Nothingness to the world of empirical things. It is to be remembered that throughout the entire system what is observable is ultimately the one single reality of existence which runs through all the stages, manifesting itself differently at each stage. Moreover, the thinkers of the *wahdat al-wujúd* school recognize no distance in terms of time between the highest stage, i.e. that of the Mystery of Mysteries or existence in its absolutely unconditional purity, and the lowest stage, i.e. that of the phenomenal or empirical things. In other words, the process by which the reality of existence goes on manifesting itself is not a process of temporal evolvement as the preceding description might have suggested. "Time" appears only at the lowest stage, i.e. in the world of empirical things. In reality, the moment we posit pure existence we must posit—at one and the same time—the phenomenal existence, just as there is no temporal discrepancy between the appearance of the sun and the appearance of light, although *essentially* light depends upon the sun, that is to say, although essentially the sun is prior and the light is posterior. Exactly the same kind of essential, i.e. non-temporal priority-posteriority relationship is recognizable between pure existence and phenomenal existence. Haydar Ámulí explains this relationship through the metaphor of the sea and the waves. The waves, he says, are ultimately nothing other than various forms assumed by the sea itself. In this sense the waves cannot subsist independently of the sea. But the sea, on its part, as long as it is sea, cannot be without waves. In each individual wave the sea appears in a different form from all others. But throughout all the different waves the reality of the sea remains one.

The important point here to remark is that, just as the waves cannot exist without the sea, so also the sea is inseparable from the waves. This would imply in a non-metaphorical language that the reality of existence is inseparable from the phenomenal things. The reality of existence cannot but manifest itself in various phenomenal forms; the original Nothingness cannot but determine itself into an infinity of divergent, concrete things. Thus is created the empirical world. Theologically we might express the same conception by saying that God out of His limitless Mercy, and because of His limitless Mercy, cannot but give Himself to all things. Existence, which spreads itself through its variously manifested forms, is called in this respect "Mercy" (*rahmah*), or the "breath of Mercifulness" (*nafas rahmání*). Ontologically the same is called *wujúd lá bi-shart qismí*, i.e. "existence as non-conditioned" which must be distinguished from *lá bi-shart maqsamí* "exist-

ence as absolutely non-conditioned" which, as we have mentioned earlier, is the Mystery of Mysteries where existence-
itself transcends even the condition of being non-conditioned.
The *lá bi-shar* or "non-conditioned" which applies to the
"breath of Mercifulness," on the contrary, means that existence in its self-manifesting and self-revealing aspect, is existence which is not determined and particularized by being exclusively attached to any particular form. Rather it is the reality considered as being capable of, and being ready to, appear
in any determined form whatsoever. Existence here is conceived as being in a special mode of indetermination in the
sense that it is the center of a limitless number of possible
determinations.

And yet, as I have repeatedly pointed out, existence is one
in whatever determined form it may appear. In this particular
sense, the whole world of Being, including both its visible and
invisible regions, is one single reality of existence. It is precisely in this sense that the people of *wahdat al-wujúd* understand the famous saying: *kána alláh wa-lam yakun ma'a-hu
shay'*, "God was, and there was nothing besides Him." This
dictum which is usually understood to refer to the state of
affairs before God created the world, is given a completely
different interpretation by the people of *wahdat al-wujúd*. According to them, this dictum must be understood as referring
to an eternal ontological truth which is valid beyond all limitations of time. The statement holds true eternally. "God was,
and there was nothing besides Him" is not a description of a
particular state of affairs before the creation of the world. It is
equally true of the situation of the world after it has been
created. In other words, "God is, and God will be; and there
is, and there will be, nothing besides Him," for in reality there
is in the whole world of Being nothing which is legitimately
entitled to be regarded as "other" (*ghayr*) than God.

The preceding analysis has thus brought to light as the basic structure of *wahdat al-wujúd* type of metaphysics four stages of existence and four ontological modes of "existence."

The four basic stages are:
(1) *Dhat al-wujúd*, existence-itself in its absolute purity.
(2) *Ahadíyah*, absolute Oneness; existence without any articulation.
(3) *Wáhidíyah*, the unity of multiplicity; existence with inner articulations; the stage of the eternal Archetypes.
(4) Phenomenal "existence."

The four modes of existence are:
(a) *Lá bi-shart maqsamí*, existence as absolutely non-conditioned.
(b) *Bi-shart lá*, existence as negatively conditioned.
(c) *Bi-shart shay'*, existence as conditioned by being-something.
(d) *Lá bi-shart qismí*, existence as relatively non-conditioned.

The correlation of these two conceptual systems one with the other may be graphically shown by the following diagram:

REALITY OF EXISTENCE
(1) Existence-itself   =(a) *la bi-shart maqsami*

(2) Oneness   = (b) *bi-shart la*   — (2)
                                              ↓ most sacred
                                                emanation   (d) *la bi-shart*
(3) Unity   ⎫   — (3)   *qismi*
                 ⎬ = (c) *bi-shart shay'*   ↓ sacred emanation
(4) Phenomena   ⎭   — (4)

NOTES

1. See, e.g., my *Sufism and Taoism: A Comparative Study of Key Philosophical Concepts* (Berkeley: University of California Press, 1984) and *Celestial Journey: Far Eastern Ways of Thinking* (Ashland, Oregon: White Cloud Press, 1995).

2. See chapter 1, pages 12-20 for a fuller discussion of the *faná'-baqá'* experience.

3. Haydar Ámulí, *Jámi' al-asrár wa-manba' al-anwár*, ed. Henry Corbin and Osman Yahya (Tehran and Paris: Bibliotheque iranien, 1969), sec. 310, 161, and sec. 397, 206-207.

4. Ibid., sec. 212, 107.

5. For more details about the structure of this triple negation, see my Eranos lecture "The Absolute and the Perfect Man in Taoism," in *Eranos Jahrbuch: 36* (Zurich: Rhein-Verlag, 1967), 426-428; and *Sufism and Taoism*, 444-454.

6. *Chung mia chih mén*; see my *Sufism and Taoism*, 398-413.

7. *Hadíth al-qudsí* is a tradition or saying in which God speaks in the first person.

8. As explained above, the *ahadíyah* is the *exterior* of the *dhát al-wujúd*, i.e. existence itself or existence in its absolute unconditionality; and it is the interior of the *wáhidíyah*. This would imply that we must distinguish in the *ahadíyah* itself two aspects turned toward opposite directions, i.e. two faces, one turned toward its own "interior" (*dhát al-wujúd*) and the other turned toward its own "exterior" (*wáhidíyah*). The same structure is found also in the *wáhidíyah*.

CHAPTER 4

MYSTICISM AND THE LINGUISTIC PROBLEM OF EQUIVOCATION IN THE THOUGHT OF 'AYN AL-QUDÁT HAMADÁNÍ

'AYN AL-QUDÁT HAMADÁNÍ (1098-1131 C.E.) stands out as a tragic figure in the history of Islamic thought. Like his great predecessor Mansúr al-Halláj (857-922 C.E.) for whose *aná'-l haqq* (I am the Absolute!) he never concealed his unreserved admiration, 'Ayn al-Qudát's "free thinking" provoked envy and hatred in the minds of the conservative orthodox theologians and lawyers, resulting in his execution as a heretic in his native town of Hamadán at the age of 33, with appalling cruelty by the hands of a Seljúqid vizier of Iraq. He was a mystic of profound spiritual experiences, and at the same time a thinker endowed with an unusually keen intellectual power of analysis. On the ground of this happy combination of mystical penetration and rational thinking, one can rightly regard him as a precursor of the long Iranian tradition of *hikmat* philosophy to be inaugurated soon after his death by Suhrawardí (1153-1191 C.E.) and Ibn 'Arabí, (1165-1210 C.E.). Here I will analyze the very original semantic aspect of the thought of this philosophic genius who has been up to a short time ago unduly neglected by the orientalists.[1]

The basic principle underlying the whole structure of Hamadání's thought, reduced to the most elementary form, will be found to consist in making a sharp distinction between knowing the reality of a thing through an immediate personal experience of it and knowing something *about* the thing. To know about honey that it is sweet is one thing, to know by experience the sweetness of honey another. The same distinction between the two types of knowledge holds true at the higher level of religious life. Thus to know something *about* God is completely different from knowing Him by coming into direct contact with the divine order of things.

'Ayn al-Qudát noticed this difference himself through a personal, and we might say, existential experience. At first he was making a most extensive study of theological works. But the study of theology caused in his mind nothing but confusion, bewilderment, and despair. A spiritual crisis came. He could only overcome it by study of the works of Abú Hámid al-Ghazálí (1058-1111 C.E.), to which he devoted four years. He did not personally meet Ghazálí, but under the latter's spiritual guidance he went to the extreme limits of intellectual power and almost went over them. Without being clearly conscious of the fact, he was gradually stepping into the supra-intellectual domain of Divine Mystery; when quite by chance he met the brother of Abú Hámid, the noted mystic master Ahmad al-Ghazálí (d. circa 1126 C.E.). It was under Ahmad Ghazálí's personal guidance that he went definitely beyond the boundaries of rational thinking far into the divine world itself where human reason and its logical function are reduced to utter powerlessness.[2]

Man's stepping into the divine world is for Hamadání an event of decisive importance consisting in the realization of a new depth of consciousness in his interior. It implies man's existential transition to an entirely different plane of consciousness from that of sensation and rational thinking. Hamadání calls this event the "opening of the eye of spiritual vision" (*infitáh 'ayn al-basírah*),[3] or "of the eye of gnostic cognition" (*'ayn al-marífah*).[4] He refers to it also by saying: "a window is opened in your interior toward the domain of the supra-sensible order of things" (*rawzanah ila 'álam al-malakút*).[5] Sometimes it is described as the "appearance of light in the interior" (*zuhúr núr fí al-bátin*).[6] Ontologically, this subjective "light" lightens up what he calls the "domain beyond reason" (*al-tawr wará'a al-'aql*).[7]

Not that Hamadání despises, or negates the value of, reason and rational thinking.[8] But man, according to him, does not reach perfection unless he goes beyond the "domain of reason," after having gone to the utmost limits of his rational power, into the trans-rational dimension of things. The very structure of the whole world of Being, in his conception, is such that the last stage of the domain of empirical experiences is directly connected with the first stage of the "domain beyond reason."[9]

After these preliminary remarks, we are now in a position to discuss the nature of the specific problems raised by Hamadání with regard to the semantic structure of human language. It goes without saying that the words and their combinations which are at our disposal are primarily so made that they might most conveniently and suitably be used for the purposes of daily communication. Our language is at its best when it is used to express and describe our experiences in the empirical world where the senses and reason fulfil their natural functions. But even in this dimension it often happens that we get embarrassed by the realization that there is a wide gap between what we feel or know and what we can say. As Ludwig Wittgenstein remarked: If someone knows how many feet high Mont Blanc is and yet is not able to say it, we naturally are surprised; but not so if someone knows how a clarinet sounds and yet is not able to say it, for the knowledge of how a clarinet sounds is not a kind of thing which can properly be described by an ordinary combination of words at our disposal.[10] And of course the situation grows far worse if, in addition to the empirical dimension of human experience, we recognize the authenticity of the supra-empirical dimension of spiritual or mystical awareness. The Sufi, when he wishes at all to express himself verbally or describe his personal visions, must of necessity be faced with all the linguistic problems that arise from the serious discrepancy between what be knows and what he can actually say.[11]

What, then, will be the effective means the Sufi can have recourse to in order to fill up this intrinsic deficiency of his linguistic apparatus? Or, is there at all any? Symbolism will perhaps be the first thing that one might think of. In fact many mystic poets—or even mystic philosophers—in all ages have created systems of symbols and taken refuge in them. But it is not symbolism that Hamadání has recourse to. Instead, he proposes that one should in such cases use words in a multi-dimensional way which he designates as *tashábuh*, or "equivocation." And in fact, according to him, the majority of the key-terms of religious philosophy in Islam must be interpreted by way of "equivocation."

However, in order that we might be able to understand the full meaning of a word used in an equivocal way—not to speak of those cases in which we ourselves are using a word in such manner—we have to have cultivated in ourselves an extremely flexible and, as it were, mobile attitude with regard to the semantic connection between a word and the meaning which it is intended to indicate.

The most serious hindrance in the way of our understanding or using words equivocally is the unduly great importance we ordinarily tend to attach to words in the word-meaning relationship. This tendency is shown in its crudest form in the infantile use of language.[12] Children in fact cannot easily identify semantically the word *layth*, for example, with *asad* simply because these words happen to have two different external forms, although in Arabic both mean one and the same thing: "lion." But the grown-ups, too, often commit fundamentally the same kind of mistake, albeit in a bit more sophisticated form.

The attitude to place undue emphasis on words as distinguished from meanings is ultimately reducible to the fact that we naturally tend to believe that there is a one-to-one correspondence between a word and its meaning. In Hamadání's view, nothing can be farther from the truth. The world of meanings is something of an infinitely delicate, flexible, and flowing nature. It has no such rigid stability as corresponds to the formal or material rigidity of words. This fact is easily observable even in our daily use of the most ordinary words, although normally it does not come up to the surface of clear consciousness.

Take, for example, the Persian word *ním*, "half." The exact meaning of the word varies in a delicate way according to whether or not quantity is made the point of reference. Let us say: The major work of Abú Hámid al-Ghazálí consists of two parts; the one half (*ním*) deals with external properties of the body while the other half (*ním*) is concerned with the properties of the mind. In such a case, the word "half" does not mean the precise quantitative half of the book, because the division is here made not in terms of quantity. Similarly, the same sentence, "Man is composed of two parts," (*ádamí do chíz ast*) indicates two entirely different divisions if we mean thereby (1) "namely, head and body," and (2) "namely, mind and body."[13] The observation of this fact—which is by no means a difficult thing to do—simply indicates that there is an undeniable discrepancy between the world of words and the world of meanings. Unfortunately, however, this semantic discrepancy is not so obvious on levels of discourse higher than that of empirical experience.

Hamadání, be it remarked at this point, does not believe that there is between a word and its meaning a strong, inner organic tie. Quite the contrary, the semantic tie between them is, in his view, something perfunctory, purely external, and in a certain sense, even unreal. For there is no equal distribution of weight between the two terms of the relationship. Only a very precarious sort of equilibrium is maintained between them. How can it be otherwise? The two, according to Hamadání, belong to different orders of being. The word belongs in the world of material and sensible things (*mulk*), while the meaning properly is of the world of immateriality (*malakút*). Compared with the vast field of meaning that lies behind each word, the latter is nothing more than an insignificant, tiny point. The word is but a narrow gate through which the human mind steps into a boundless domain of meaning. Moreover, the meaning is something that has, so to speak, its own life. It has no fixity. Quite independently of the word which indicates it, the meaning develops as it were of its own accord with amazing flexibility in accordance with the degree of depth of man's experience and consciousness. The meaning with such characteristics is poured into the ready-made mould of a word. By simply observing from outside the word thus employed, one could hardly judge the width and depth of the meaning that is intended to be conveyed by it. This is particularly true when the meaning that has been poured into the mould of a word happens to be backed by a profound mystical experience. When the meaning is thus of a non-empirical nature, the use of a word in reference to it necessarily goes to the extremity of equivocation (*ghāyat al-tashābuh*).[14]

In such cases, in order to gain an exact insight into the meaning indicated, one has to take a very delicate attitude towards the indicating word. For one is here required to use the given word as a springboard by which to dive into the depth of the meaning. As long as one remains trying to understand the meaning *from* the word, one can never hope to obtain it. Rather at the very first and the slightest touch with the word, one must leave it there and go directly into the domain of meaning.[15] But in order to understand the real significance of this idea, we must first elucidate the structure of equivocation according to what Hamadāní says about it.

"Equivocation" or "equivocality" (*tashābuh*) normally implies uncertainty, indetermination, and ambiguousness in the use of a word. The ultimate source of these negative properties is polysemy, a semantic phenomenon in which a word happens to have in its basic structure a number of different meanings. If, for instance, the Arabic word *'ayn* is used without any clarifying context, or within an insufficiently clear context, one is said to be using the word equivocally. For *'ayn* can mean such widely divergent things as "eye," "spring" (source of water), "essence," "gold piece," "uterine brother," etc.

The kind of equivocation Hamadāní is thinking of is completely different from this type of polysemy. For the divergent meanings that are connected with a word like *'ayn* stand in one and the same dimension. It is, we might say, a case of horizontal polysemy, while what Hamadání is concerned with may be characterized as vertical polysemy. The latter is the multidimensional structure of meaning based upon the multi-dimensional use of the word.

Thus the equivocation as conceived by Hamadání refers to those cases in which one and the same word—one and the same expression—happens to be used *significantly* and *at the same time* at two or more than two different levels of discourse. There are conceivable many such levels of discourse, but Hamadání is interested principally in two of them: [A] the level of rational thinking, and [B] the level of the domain beyond reason to which reference has earlier been made.

The [A] level is linguistically no other than a linear extension of the ordinary use of language in the daily, empirical dimension of human experience. In the particular context which is our immediate concern, the [A] level refers primarily to the linguistic expression of theological concepts and thinking. Just to give an example in a preliminary way, the theologians often speak of the "nearness" (*qurb*) and "remoteness" (*bu'd*) of man from God. Thus, for instance, those who do not believe in God are said to be "remote" from Him, while the believers are said to be "close" to, or "near" God. As such, it is a perfectly significant use of the words. The concepts of "nearness" and "remoteness" in this context are but the result of the theological elaboration of the "nearness" and "remoteness" respectively of the sensible things which we encounter in our daily empirical experiences. Consequently, these two concepts are at this level still understood basically in terms of the image or idea of spatial distance.

However, the same words, *qurb* and *bu'd*, can be, and are in fact often used by the mystics in describing the content of their peculiar intuitions, whether religious or metaphysical. In such a case, the words—according to the basic pattern of analysis which we have here adopted—are being used at the [B] level. The most important point to note concerning the [B] level is that the meaning which is actualized at this stage can never be reached no matter how far one may extend the meaning that obtains at the [A] level. This comes from the fact that the meanings of all words at the [B] level are based on cognitive experiences that are of a radically different nature from what is experienced in the dimension of rational thinking, not to speak of in the dimension of daily life. For, as we have seen above, the meanings at the [B] level are perceived only by the "eye of spiritual vision" in the "domain beyond reason." Thus, for example, *qurb* (nearness) at this level means for Hamadání a certain supra-sensible relationship that obtains between all existents and the Source of existence, a very peculiar relationship, the structure of which will be analyzed in detail later on. Suffice it to say at this stage that "nearness" here means the relationship of absolute ontological equality which all things bear to God. Taking the word "distance" in an non-spatial sense, Hamadání often speaks of all things standing at an absolutely equal distance from God.[16] Although Hamadání himself does not explicitly analyze the meaning of "remoteness" at the [B] level, it is clear that, since there is no spatial reference in this domain, "remoteness" turns out to be exactly of the same meaning as "nearness," i.e. all things being at the same (non-spatial) "distance" from God.

Although, in this way, the same word, "nearness," has two entirely different meanings, we should not commit the mistake of thinking that the meaning [A] and the meaning [B] have nothing to do with each other. The relation between the meaning [A] and the meaning [B] is not at all the same as the one which obtains between, say, "fountain," "eye," "gold," "essence," etc. as possible meanings of the word *'ayh*. For even at the [B] level, *qurb* does mean "nearness." Only the "nearness" that is actualized in the supra-sensible dimension is of a totally different structure from the "nearness" in the sensible or rational dimension of experience. Otherwise expressed, the semantic content of "nearness" changes from spatial to non-spatial in accordance with the qualitative change that occurs in the human consciousness. But this change does not affect the fact that one and the same word is being used significantly and meaningfully at two different levels, [A] and [B].

The question is not : Which of the two meanings—[A] or [B]—is genuine and real? (or which is figurative and metaphorical?) For both are equally authentic and real, each in its peculiar dimension, because each is backed by an authentic experience. When I say, for example, "I see a flower," my *seeing* has on the empirical level an authentic meaning backed by an authentic sense experience. Likewise, when I say, "The whole is bigger than a part of it," my statement has an authentic meaning at the level of rational thinking (the [A] level). In the same way, when Mansúr al-Halláj says *aná'l-haqq*, "I am the Absolute," his statement has an authentic meaning at the supra-sensible and supra-rational level of experience (the [B] level).[17] The only important point is that each of these three sentences must be understood strictly in terms of the dimension to which it properly belongs.

To have this kind of understanding, however, with regard to words and sentences belonging to the [B] level is extremely difficult, if not absolutely impossible. For *aná'l-haqq* of al-Halláj, *subhání*, "Glory to me," of Bastámí, and the like are all inspired utterances made by mystics of the highest spiritual calibre when they happen to be in an unusual state of consciousness—a state in which their rational power has broken

down and in which they have been "annihilated in the illumination of the overpowering Light of eternity."

> Here there is no more the subject of knowledge left; the act
> of knowing itself has been annihilated; and everything has
> turned into the object of knowledge (which is properly speak-
> ing no longer the *object* of knowledge, since there is no sub-
> ject to know it). It is in such a state that this remaining point
> discloses itself in the plain of pure and absolute Divinity
> (*jabarút*). Then what could Husayn (al-Halláj) say but *aná'l-
> haqq*! What could Báyazíd (Bastámí) say but *subhání*.[18]

It will be clear that in order that one might be able to
understand the meaning of such utterances strictly in terms of
the [B] level to which they belong, one has to have passed
through the same kind of mystical experience.

Consequently, for those who have no direct experiential
knowledge of the domain beyond reason the use of words at
the [B] level—even if they theoretically admit the legitimacy
of such use of words—must necessarily appear as figurative.[19]
Briefly stated, words used at the [B] level are for the majority
of men metaphors. The word *núr*, "light," for instance, is for
them simply a metaphor when God is called Light.

For those who have direct access to the "domain beyond
reason," however, it is rather the meaning at the [A] level (i.e.
núr in the sense of physical light) that is metaphorical. This
because the dimension of [B] is precisely the Place where
reality is experienced in its original, absolute state. In this
particular context the [A] use of language is metaphorical,
while the [B] use is real.[20]

As a typical example illustrating the semantic structure of
language at the [A] and [B] level, we shall now take up the
word *'ilm*, "knowledge," as it appears in the phrase "God's
knowledge," about which Hamadání himself goes into con-

siderable detail. As in the foregoing, let [A] represent the theological and [B] the supra-rational, or mystical level of understanding.

At the [A] level which is, as noted before, but a theological extension of the ordinary use of language, "God knows something" is naturally understood on the analogy of "Man knows something." And within the confines of this understanding various theological problems are raised and discussed by the theologians under the title of the "divine attributes" for the knowledge in this context is conceived as one of the attributes of God.

Since the meaning of a word as understood at the [A] level is essentially and ultimately nothing other than a theoretic extension or elaboration of the empirical, pre-theological understanding of the same word, so 'ilm (knowledge) too, is naturally understood on the analogy of what is usually understood by the word in ordinary daily circumstances. Now in the ordinary, empirical dimension, "knowledge" has a peculiar structure of its own based on a two-term relation between the subject ('alim, the knower) and the object (ma'lūm, the known). And what is peculiar about this cognitive relationship consists in the fact that the subject is passive and the object active. That is to say, the subject of knowledge can play the role of a subject when and only when there is something to be known. The existence of the object precedes the existence of the subject qua subject: $(S \leftarrow O)$.[21]

This peculiar structure of empirical knowledge is transferred consciously or unconsciously to the theological plane of thinking. Thus the theological proposition "God knows X" would be understood in the following sense: There is first X as a possible object of divine knowledge, and that God comes to know it as it really is. God does have an attribute called knowledge but it can exercise its function only when there are proper objects to be known. The object, in short, acts upon, and determines, the subject. Hence the notorious *aporia* concerning God's knowledge of the particulars, i.e. the individual things and events of the empirical world.

This *aporia* arises when, on the assumption that knowledge at all levels of experience maintains the above-mentioned basic structure (S←O), we ask the theological question whether God knows the particulars. If we say, "Yes," we would thereby be implying that God's knowledge is something contingent. For the empirical world is by nature a domain of contingency. All things are there constantly changing. No particular thing remains exactly the same for two units of time. If God's knowledge is to pursue the particular things as they go on changing from moment to moment, it must also go on changing from moment to moment. Moreover, in this world new things incessantly come into being, and new states of affairs are constantly occurring. According as God becomes aware of them, new cognitive states would have to occur constantly in His mind. But to admit this would be nothing other than admitting the contingency of God's knowledge.[22]

If, in order to escape this difficulty, we say, "No," we would simply be saying that God is ignorant of certain things. Where then would be the omniscience of God? Curiously enough, this statement of God's ignorance, namely the proposition: "The knowledge of the Eternal does not comprehend the particulars of the [empirical] world" (*'ilm-e azal be-juz'iyát-e 'alam muhíl níst*) was precisely one of the statements for the sake of which Hamadání was accused of heresy and unbelief.[23]

According to Hamadání, the above *aporia* itself arises simply because the theologians understand the meaning of "knowledge" on the analogy of what is meant by the same world in the empirical dimension of experience. This way of understanding appears as something quite natural in the light of what we have said earlier about the semantic structure of the [A] level; namely, that the use of language at this level is but a theological extension of the empirical use of language. The theologians are after all people who cannot break the magic spell of ordinary language.

In order, however, to grasp the real semantic structure of God's knowledge, one will have to push one's analysis further beyond the confines of ordinary rational thinking into the intermediary region lying between the [A] level and [B] level.[24] More concretely stated, one will have to have recourse to a peculiar type of thinking which is at once rational reasoning and metaphysical intuition. This will be done in the following way.

A distinction must be made, first of all, between two kinds of knowledge: (1) knowledge which presupposes, and is derived from, the existence of the object to be known, and (2) knowledge which is presupposed by, and from which is derived, the very existence of the object known. Hamadání explains this distinction by an example taken from the domain of daily experience. "My knowledge about this epistle (which I am now sending to you) had been there in my mind before I actually began writing it. And this knowledge of mine was the cause of the existence of this epistle. If it were not for this knowledge that is the cause of the existence of your knowledge."[25] The relation between God's knowledge and the particulars must be understood as of the same structure as the relation which holds in this example between "my knowledge" and "this epistle of mine."

Thus through the basic distinction made between the two kinds of knowledge, Hamadání's thought approaches the metaphysical dimension of things. He concludes:

The knowledge of the Eternal is the very "Source of exist-

ence" (*yanbú'-e wujúd*). All existents, whether of the empirical world or of the supra-empirical world, are to the infinite
width of God's eternal knowledge just as one single letter (of
one single word) appearing in this epistle is to the width of
my knowledge and ability.[26]

From this conclusion to the highest level of discourse
(level [B]) it is only a matter of one further step. But on the
other hand there is also noticeable a remarkable difference
between the [B] level and the preceding levels, whether [A] or
the intermediary. For even at the intermediary stage which has
just been described and which is evidently very much of a
metaphysical or ontological nature, the word "knowledge" still
retains something of an epistemological connotation. There
is, in other words, in the use of the term "knowledge" still
some reference, no matter how slight it may be, to the ordinary mental activity of man by which he perceives and knows
objective things. As used at the [B] level, on the contrary,
"knowledge" carries absolutely no epistemological connotation. Its meaning is purely metaphysical. For God's knowledge here means God's *ma'iyah* (literally "withness" or the
absolute non-separation of God from all things), and consequently the equidistance of all things from their ultimate ontological Source. This is an interesting point which needs to
be elucidated in some detail, because Hamadání himself declares that it is his original idea and that nobody has ever
expressed such a view on this problem.[27]

It is a matter of common experience, he begins to argue,
that we constantly find things in the empirical world standing
in priority-posteriority relationship to each other. The appearance of the sunbeams, for example, comes after the rise of
the sun, the latter being the cause of the former. Likewise, the
movement of the pen with which I am now writing these

words follows the movement of my hand, which again follows the existence of myself as the writer.

The structure of the events of this kind, however, will appear in a completely different light when looked at from the point of view of the divine dimension. For in this perspective, both the sun and its beams are found to be standing at an equal distance from the Absolute. In a similar way, (1) the pen which is an instrument by which I am writing, (2) the letters written by me and (3) the writer (i.e. myself) stand on one single plane and at equal distance from the Absolute. All this because we are now in a metaphysical region where there is no temporal succession (*túl*, literally "length," vertical order), between things. All things are here contemplated co-existing in a limitless, a-temporal expanse (*'ard*, literally "breadth," horizontal order) of existence.

Hamadání criticizes Ibn Síná by saying that the latter has confused the empirical dimension with the divine dimension when he has established his proof of the existence of God on the causal connections between things. A thing *A*, in order to exist, must have something else, *B*, as its cause; *B* in its turn must have its own cause *C*; *C* must have *D*, etc. . . And at the very extremity of the whole series of causes, A--B--C--D. . ., Ibn Síná believes to have found the Cause of all causes, God the Absolute.

According to Hamadání this view is completely wrong. He points out the crucial weakness of Ibn Síná's argument in the following way.

> There are in this epistle of mine, for example, ten thousand letters. Each letter comes into being (i.e. is written) after another letter. And the second line comes after the first line; the third line after the second; the fourth after the third. Now suppose someone says: The tenth line comes into being from

the ninth; the ninth from the eighth; the eighth from the seventh, etc., and finally the third from the second, the second from the first. Suppose further that at this point he says: The first line itself has come into being from the will and ability (to write) of the writer. This person evidently is taking a wrong view of the matter, because he is seeking the position of the writer in the vertical (i.e. temporal) evolvement of the epistle, instead of in the horizontal (i.e. a-temporal) expanse of it. Such a person will no doubt consider the distance of the first and the second line from the will of the writer much shorter than the distance of the eighth, ninth, or tenth line from his will to write).[28]

We have only to apply this kind of thinking to the above mentioned argument of Ibn Sīná to realize that the mistake committed by him consists precisely in that he is (unconsciously) representing God as something temporal (*zamání*).

If he had been in possession of a pure, uncontaminated view, he would have seen no distance between God and any contingent thing; he would have recognized the existential equidistance of all things from Him. For the Absolute absolutely transcends time. Witness how all the letters that are written on this sheet of paper stand at an equal distance from the writer, if they are considered from the viewpoint of the a-temporal existential expanse, not from that of temporal succession.[29]

This existential equidistance of all things from God is the semantic structure of the word *'ilm* (knowledge) as it is used at the [B] level of discourse in reference to the divine attribute which is indicated by the same word. There still remains one more point to mention concerning the structure of "withness"

(God is *with* all things). It will be obvious that "withness" implies the existence of a certain relation between the Absolute and the empirical things. But it is a very peculiar kind of relation. The peculiarity consists in the fact that this relation has actuality only when looked at from the side of the Absolute, but not from the side of the things. For the things in the empirical world are in themselves sheer "nothing," having no reality of their own. The reality or existence that they seem to have is derived from the very relation into which they enter by the activity of the Absolute.[30]

Thus in terms of our ordinary use of the word "relation" (*nisbah*), the relation which we are now taking about is no relation at all. How could there be any relation when one of the terms of relation is "nothing "? This is precisely what is meant by Hamadání when he says: "Everything that exists in this world has a relation to the width of the eternal knowledge, but this relation is so to speak the relation which a "nothing" (*lá-shay'*) bears to a thing which is infinite."[31] But to say so is tantamount to saying that "no existent thing has any relation whatsoever to the width of the eternal Knowledge."[32] Therefore, we can rightly say: God is *with* the things, but we cannot reverse the order and say: The things are with God.[33] For there is absolutely nothing in the world that could stand face to face with God. It is God that turns His Face (*wahj*) to all things, and that is the real meaning of the statement that God knows all things.[34] The things themselves have no face to turn toward God.

Since, however, it is impossible in normal circumstances to think of, or to represent, a two-term relation with "nothing" as one of its terms, we tend to imagine "nothing" as "something" and posit between the two terms a bilateral relationship (A↔B). Thus we often speak of the things standing in front of God, turning their faces toward Him (*muqábalah*).[35]

But, on the other hand, it is also true that the things do possess a certain kind of reality which is derived from God's turning His Face toward them. In this sense there is a bilateral relationship between the things and God. And in this perspective, each of the existents in the world is "existent" (*mawjúd*) and "non-existent" (*ma'dúm*) at one and the same time. It is this peculiar ontological situation that the word "knowledge" (of God) indicates at the [B] level of discourse. The phenomenon of equivocation as understood by Hamadání consists in a multidimensional structure formed by two or more meanings (as those of the word "knowledge" at the [A] and [B] levels), which are different from each other in terms of the depth of vision, being put together into one single semantic entity.

NOTES

1. The study is based on three of Hamadání's major works that have been edited and published in Teheran: *Zubdat al-haqá'iq* (Arabic) ed. 'Afif 'Oseyrán, 1962; *Tamhídát* (Persian) ed. 'Afif 'Oseyrán, 1962; *Náme-há-ye 'Ayn al-Qudát Hamadání* "Epistles" (Persian), ed. 'Afif 'Oseyrán and 'Alinaqí Munzawí, 1969. It is my pleasant duty to add that in the course of preparing this paper I have profited much by valuable suggestions made by Professor Hermann Landolt of the Institute of Islamic Studies, McGill University.

2. This whole process of spiritual development is described with a beautiful touch of lyricism by 'Ayn al-Qudat himself in *Zubdat al-haqá'iq*, 6-7.

3. Ibid.,7, and passim.

4. Ibid., 30.

5. Ibid., 58.

6. Ibid., 26.

7. Ibid., 27, and passim. It is one of the technical expressions

that appear constantly in Hamadání's writings. It is also called the "domain (that comes) after reason" (*al-tawr alladhí ba'da al-'aql*).

8. Cf. ibid., 10.

9. Cf. ibid., 35.

10. Ludwig Wittgenstein, *Philosophical Investigations.* Translated by G.E.M. Anscombe (New York: MacMillan, 1953), 36.

11. *Zubdat al-haqá'iq,* 88.

12. *Epistle,* No. LX, sec. 753, 452.

13. *Epistle,* No. LIII, sec. 677, 405.

14. *Zubdat al-haqá'iq,* 4.

15. Ibid., 58.

16. Ibid., 77-78.

17. For an analysis of the famous Hallajian statement, see *Shakwa al-gharíb,* ed. 'Afif 'Oseyrán, (Teheran, 1962), 36, 62. Arberry's English translation: *A Sufi Martyr* (London, 1969), 36, and *Tamhídát,*, sec. 84, 62; sec. 108, 77; sec. 104, 75.

18. *Tamhídát,* sec. 84, 62. Cf. *Epistle* No. XLII, sec. 560, 355, where the expression "the plain of *mulk*" (i.e. empirical dimension) is used instead of "the plain of *jabarút.*" Both expressions make good sense, because the mystical experience in question belongs to the dimension of *jabarút,* but its *linguistic* expression is actualized only in the empirical wolrld.

19. *Zubdat al-haqá'iq,* 24.

20. Ibid., 21-22.

21. *Epistle,* XXI, sec. 270, 176-177.

22. *Zubdat al-haqá'iq,*, 22, 25. See also chapter 2 of this book, "The Paradox of Light and Darkness in the Garden of Mysteries of Shabastarí" pp. 39-66, for a discussion of "light and darkness" in Sufi thought.

23. *Epistle,* VIII, sec. 219, 150.

24. 'Ayn al-Qudát himself does not speak of the "intermediary region" between [A] and [B]. Theoretically he seems to he content with his distinction between the two levels of discourse, so that according to his own description the analysis here in question would seem to be made still within the conflnes of theological

thinking. But for the sake of clarity we had better, I think, consider it as something going beyond the [A] dimension.

25. *Epistle*, VIII, sec. 220, 150-151.

26. Ibid., XIX, sec. 251, 166.

27. Ibid., sec. 22, 20.

28. Ibid., sec. 23, 21.

29. Ibid.

30. In the terminology of the later theosophers, this kind of relation is called "illuminative relation" (*idáfah ishráqíyah*)

31. *Zubdat al-haqá'iq*, 21.

32. Ibid., 25.

33. Ibid., 62-63, 76.

34. Ibid., 20, 26.

35. Ibid., 23.

CHAPTER 5

CREATION AND THE TIMELESS ORDER OF THINGS: A STUDY IN THE MYSTICAL PHILOSOPHY OF 'AYN AL-QUDÁT AL-HAMADÁNÍ

'**A**YN AL-QUDÁT AL-HAMADÁNÍ, whose name was once almost totally obliterated from the pages of the history of Islamic philosophy, has recently been resuscitated out of oblivion and his importance is beginning to be duly recognized among those who are interested in the philosophic aspects of Sufism. However, no systematic study of the thought of this remarkable mystic-philosopher has yet been undertaken.

Hamadání closed his short, tragic life in Hamadán in an age which just preceded the appearance of Ibn 'Arabí and Suhrawardí,[1] two outstanding figures in the history of Islamic thought, of whom he may rightly be regarded as a precursor. He deserves this peculiar position for two obvious reasons. Firstly, he, as a thinker, unified in himself Sufism and scholastic philosophy. A disciple of Ahmad al-Ghazálí, he was in fact

CREATION AND THE TIMELESS ORDER OF THINGS

a living embodiment of the tradition of profound mystical experiences that had come down to him under the name of Sufism (*tasawwuf*) represented by such names as Halláj and Báyazíd Bastámí. He was at the same time an intellectual endowed with an unusually keen power of rational analysis which enabled him to philosophize on the basis of his own spiritual visions.

Secondly, in metaphysics he stands closest to Ibn 'Arabí, not only in the sense that his metaphysical thinking is strictly dictated by and in accordance with his mystical experience but in the sense that his position shows a striking structural similarity to what is known as the thesis of the "unity of existence" (*wahdat al-wujúd*) on which Ibn 'Arabí established the whole edifice of his mystical metaphysics. In this respect Hamadání was uncontestedly a forerunner of Ibn 'Arabí.

These considerations—which may readily be developd into a number of long articles concerning the historical relationship between these men—would seem to suggest that it is possible for us to follow historically the spirit of Hamadání as it goes through the Master of illuminationism (Suhrawardí) and the *Magister Maximus* of the unity of existence (Ibn 'Arabí), and develops into a peculiar type of theosophic philosophy that has come to be known in the latter phases of Islamic thought, and particularly in Iran, as *Hikmat*-philosophy.[2]

In this chapter I will examine the basic pattern of thinking which characterizes Hamadání as a mystic-philosopher, through a concrete example, namely by examining the peculiar way in which he dealt with the Islamic concept of creation.[3]

II

What characterizes Hamadání's pattern of thinking in a most striking manner is that his thought is structured in reference to two different levels of cognition at one and the same time.

That is to say, the process of philosophic thinking[4] in Hamadání is as a rule related to two levels of discourse, one referring to the domain of empirical experience based on sensation and rational interpretation, and the other referring to a totally different kind of understanding which is peculiar to the "domain beyond reason." There is admittedly nothing new in this distinction itself. For almost all mystics naturally tend to distinguish between what is accessible to sensation and reason and what lies beyond the grasp of all forms of empirical cognition. Otherwise they would not be worthy to be specifically called "mystics." What is really characteristic of Hamadání is rather that everything—i.e. every event, every state of affairs, or every concept which deserves being discussed in a philosophic way—is spoken of in terms of these two essentially incompatible levels of discourse. All the major concepts that have been sanctioned by tradition as authentically Islamic, whether they be philosophic or theological, are to be discussed and elaborated on these two levels of discourse in such a manner that each of these concepts might be shown to have an entirely different inner structure as it is viewed in reference to either of the two levels.

It is noteworthy that Hamadání does not simply and lightly dispose of reason. He ascribes to reason whatever properly belongs to it. In human life reason has its important function to fulfill; it has its own proper domain in which it maintains its sovereignty.[5] In fact he visualizes the "domain of reason" (*tawr al-'aql*)[6] and the "domain beyond reason" (*tawr wará'a al-'aql*)[7] as two contiguous regions, the latter being directly consecutive to the former.[8] This means that the last stage of the "domain of reason" is in itself the first stage of the "domain beyond reason" by having exhausted all the rational resources of thinking, are able to step into the domain of trans-rational faculty of the mind. This latter domain discloses itself to man when, at the extremity of his rational power, an all-illuminating light suddenly emerges in his interior. The appearance of this "inner light" (*núr fí al-bátin*)[9] transforms the vision of the world into something which man has never dreamt of. He is now an *'árif*, a gnostic, whereas he has been—being confined within the "domain of reason"—an *'álim*, a rational thinker. The former term designates a man who perceives by the help of his "inner light" the hidden, i.e. trans-empirical, structure of things. Henceforth his philosophy, if he does philosophize at all, will be characterized by his double vision of the world—the world as it appears to him as an *'álim* or a rational thinker, and the same world as it reveals itself to him as an *'árif*. The characteristic feature of Hamadání's thought to which reference was made at the outset can be accounted for in terms of this kind of double vision of the world.

The "domain beyond reason," according to Hamadání, is of a peculiar nature; it is structured in quite a different manner from the "domain of reason." Nevertheless the two domains are not unrelated with each other. Quite the contrary; the "domain of reason," in the view of Hamadání, is but a pale reflection of the "domain beyond reason." The true reality of things is disclosed only in the latter domain, while the former presents a distorted or disfigured picture of the same reality, the distortion being due to an action which is inevitably exerted by the cognitive patterns peculiar to reason and sensation. But no matter how pale and distorted a picture it may be, it *is* still a picture of reality. And in that sense the two domains are closely connected with one another. That is to say, for every important event or state of affairs found in the "domain of reason" we may be sure to find its original form in the other domain.

Thus, in the view of Hamadání, there is a general and

fundamental correspondence between the "domain of reason" and "the domain beyond reason," but far more remarkable is the discrepancy between them in terms of the pictures of reality they present to us. The cleavage is so wide and deep that in the majority of cases the correspondence is hardly perceptible. Hence the difficulty with which we are faced when we decide to investigate philosophically the basic make-up of reality fixing our sight upon the state of affairs in both these domains at one and the same time. Moreoever, human language is so made that its vocabulary and syntactic rules are primarily adjusted to the structure of the "domain of reason." The words and sentences by means of which we describe things—or think about them—are not naturally focused on the "domain beyond reason." Thus a mystic who, in the capacity of a philosopher, wants to talk about something he has observed in the latter domain, finds himself forced to use the linguistic tool specifically prepared for describing the things belonging to the "domain of reason."

According to Hamadání, two ways are open for the mystic to take in such a situation. Either (1) he has recourse to "equivocation" (*tashábuh*),[10] using one and the same word in two widely different senses as it refers to the one or the other domain; or (2) he describes the two corresponding states of affairs using for each of them an entirely different set of words and sentences. In his book *Zubdat al-haqá'iq*, Hamadání uses both these methods. It goes without saying that when he chooses the second alternative the interpretation on our part becomes a subtle and difficult matter, for in such a case we are liable to be misled into thinking that he is talking about two completely unrelated things. The concept of "creation" which constitutes the main topic of the present paper is just a case in point. "Creation" (*ijád*) is the key-word he uses in reference to the "domain of reason," while the same fundamental event is talked about in terms of "God's Face" (*wajh alláh*) when he looks at the matter from the point of view of the "domain beyond reason." "Creation" and "God's Face" would superficially appear to have almost nothing to do with each other. For Hamadání, however, there is between the two a remarkable structural correspondence, the main difference between them consisting in the fact that the one properly belongs to the "domain of reason" and the other to the "domain beyond reason."

III

The concept of creation is something easily accessible to ordinary rational understanding. Let us begin by examining what Hamadání has to say about it in reference to the "domain of reason."

It is to be remarked that on this level of thinking Hamadání readily accepts, at least at the initial stage, the fundamental ideas that have been developd by theologians and philosophers concerning God's creation of the world of being. Thus he starts by dividing all existent things into two major categories: "pre-eternal" (*qadím*) and "originated" (*hádith*). The pre-eternal—which in reality is a unit class, consisting as it does of one single member, namely, the Necessary Existent—is a class of existents for whose existence there is no temporal beginning. An originated, in contrast, is an existent having for its existence a temporal beginning. Creation in this context may be defined as something being brought into existence at a certain definite point of time.[11] This conception of creation is a commonplace among theologians. By itself it does not play a very conspicuous role in Hamadání's thought.

There is another understanding of the distinction between the pre-eternal and originated, which is cherished by philosophers and which Hamadání himself adopts and develops in an important way. According to this second understanding, the pre-eternal means "that which does not require for its existence any cause," whereas the originated means "that which requires for its existence a special cause."[12] Nothing except God can come into existence without an existence-giving cause ('illa mújida). As there are innumerable things in the world, there are correspondingly innumerable causes working there, but they are all ultimately reducible to the Cause of all causes, God. Creation in this context means that something that has been in the negative state of non-existence comes into the positive state of existence through the activity of its Cause. This conception of creation is also a commonplace in Islamic thought.

It should be noted that whether we adopt the first understanding or the second, creation at this stage is invariably regarded as a temporal event. In the view of Hamadání, however, the deep structural meaning which underlies this kind of common-sense understanding of creation is solely that Something (ma'ná) which, "when viewed outside of the veils of mystery, is called God (alláh) in the common parlance of the Arabs,"[13] is the ultimate source of all existent things in all their exuberant colors and forms. But God's being the ultimate source of all things is not necessarily a temporal event. Rather it has in itself nothing to do with time. It is only at the level of empirical cognition that this originally atemporal state of affairs evolves as a temporal event in accordance with the essential requirement coming from the peculiar structure of our reason and sensation. In the "domain beyond reason" it reveals itself as something entirely different from creation understood as a temporal event. This point will be fully discussed later on. For the time being, let us remain in the "domain of reason" and pursue the development of Hamadání's thought on this level of discourse.

We have seen above how the term "originated" is interpreted as "that which has (or needs) for its existence a cause." Now Islamic philosophers are unanimous in calling this kind of thing "possible" (*mumkin*, pl. *mumkinát*). A "possible" thing is everything that has in itself no ground for its own existence. In a loose sense Hamadání also calls all things in this world "possible," meaning thereby exactly what other philosophers mean by the word "possible."[14] On closer scrutiny, however, he finds this common conception of the "possible" quite inaccurate and not sufficiently elaborated. And this observation provides him with an occasion to develop his own original idea about ontological possibility.

There is a general agreement among philosophers that ontological possibility stands opposed to ontological necessity on the one hand, and to ontological impossibility on the other.

Now, if we combine the two different definitions of creation that were given above, it may be redefined as something coming into existence through the activity of its cause at a certain point in time. The thing, before coming into the state of existence, is, of course, in the state of non-existence. But as long as a thing remains in the state of non-existence, it is "impossible" to exist. This is Hamadání's understanding of ontological impossibility. However, at the very moment when it comes into the state of existence and turns into an actually existent thing, the thing becomes "necessary" to exist, that is to say, it is necessarily existent. Where, then, is the place left for possibility? It is only to be found in the imaginary point where the thing turns from the state of non-existence to the state of existence. The thing is "possible" just for a fraction of a moment which in reality is reducible to nullity.

Hamadání clarifies this rather unusual conception of ontological possibility by comparing its structure to that of the "present" which is in his view also nothing but an imaginary point between the past and the future—a typically Ghazalian conception of the present, comparable to the famous view of Saint Augustine in the West. Here follow Hamadání's own words about this problem:

> Thus the boundary of the 'necessary' is directly contiguous to the boundary of the 'impossible', there being between the two absolutely no intervening space. The only thing that serves as a line of demarcation between them is the 'possible'. But the latter in truth has no reality at all; it is just like a mathematical point ideally posted on a straight line. It is comparable also to the boundary-line separating the past from the future in the structure of time. In fact, the end of the past is directly connected with the beginning of the future. As for the boundary-line between them, it has no reality except in imagination. For if you posit in imagination a point on the line of time and divide it into the past and the future, you will find on the whole stretch of the line nothing physically distinguishable from the past and the future, nothing which you might point out as really constituting the boundary between the two segments. For it is nothing but a point posited there by imagination.[15]

The upshot of this argument is that there is in actuality no ontological possibility, and that, therefore, everything is either "impossible" or "necessary." What is generally considered "possible" is but an imaginary boundary-line separating the "impossible" from the "necessary."

Our next question is: What does Hamadání exactly mean when he declares that whatever is not yet existent is "impossible to exist" (*muhál al-wujúd*)? In an Islamic context—and such is precisely the context in which Hamadání discusses his problems—this question is of vital importance because it is immediately connected with the question of Divine Power (*qudra*). Besides, one of the most widely accepted philosophic principles states that whenever and wherever there is a complete cause the effect must necessarily come into being, just as the movement of the hand necessarily causes the movement of the ring on one of its fingers, and that without any discrepancy between the two in terms of time. How, then, does it come about that a thing comes into existence today while another thing remains in the state of non-existence until tomorrow in spite of the fact that the most complete Cause of existence is always there?[16]

Hamadání defines ontological impossibility in terms of the "lack of the (necessary) condition (*faqd shart*)." A thing remains in the state of nonexistence despite the eternal existence of its Cause, as long as the "condition" (*shart*) for existence is not actualized. Man—to explain the matter through an ordinary example—is naturally endowed with the power to speak. This power (*qudra*) is the cause of his speaking after silence. But despite the existence of this power in him, he may remain silent. In other words, the cause exists but the effect does not. This discrepancy between the cause and the effect is due not to any defect in the cause itself but to the lack of the necessary condition for the production of the expected effect, which is in this case the will (*mashí'a*) to speak. Similarly, the stars while veiled by a cloud remain invisible even if the power of sight exists in us in a perfect state. The stars being invisible in no wise indicate that our power of sight is defective. On this analogy, a thing which is still in the state of non-existence is, so to speak, covered by the veil of the non-actualization of the necessary condition. And as long as the thing is veiled by the non-actualization of the condition, the Cause (i.e. the Divine Power) does not bring it into existence—not because of any defect ascribable to the Cause itself. It is in this sense that a thing which is still non-existent is said to be "impossible" to exist. As soon as, however, the veil is removed, it turns into the state of possibility, and by that very act turns into the state of necessity.[17]

By this concept of ontological "condition" Hamadání explains the distinction which is usually made by philosophers between two sorts of impossibility: the "impossible by itself" (*muhál bi-dháti-hi*) and the "impossible by something else" (*muhál bi-ghayri-hi*). The "impossible by itself" is everything which stands to Divine Power in the same relation as an odor does to the organ of sight; an object of smell can never be an object of sight, not because of any defect in the organ of sight, but simply and solely because it is not by essence anything to be seen. Thus the "impossible by itself" is never given existence by Divine Power, not because the latter is defective in any respect, but because such a thing is by essence not in a position to become an object of Power. In terms of the concept of "condition," this may be expressed by saying that the "impossible by itself" is that for which an ontological condition can never be actualized.[18]

The "impossible by something else" on the contrary—and this is the kind of "impossible" which we have been discussing in the foregoing paragraphs—stand to divine Power in the same relation as an object of sight does to the organ of sight as long as that object remains veiled by something. Formulated in a more technical manner, the "impossible by something else" is that whose "condition" is actualizable, but not necessarily to be actualized."[19] In reference to the positive aspect of the "impossible by something else"—by the "positive aspect" is meant the "condition" for existence being actualizable. Hamadání sometimes calls it the "possible by itself" (*mumkin bi-dháti-hi*)[20] so that we have the equivalence: "impossible by something else" = "possible by itself." It is to be noted that the word "possible" is here used to mean something different from the "possible" conceived as an imaginary point between non-existence and existence.

It is also important to remark that in the opinion of Hamadání the need for the ontological "condition" does not detract from the perfection of the Cause. For it is something essentially of a negative nature. It is not to be conceived as something positive filling up the deficiency of the Cause. It consists merely in removing the veil. The dispersion of clouds enables the earth to receive the light of the sun; it works upon the natural capacity of the earth, but it does not affect in any way the activity of the sun. In like manner an ontological "condition" takes off the veil from the thing in the state of non-existence in such a way that the thing becomes ready to receive the light of eternal Existence (*núr al-wujúd al-azalí*).[21] The "condition" concerns the capacity or "preparedness" (*istidád*) of the thing; it has nothing to do with the nature of the Cause.

As to what precisely such an ontological "condition" is in more concrete terms and as to how it becomes actualized, Hamadání unfortunately does not give us any explanation in *Zubdat al-haqá'iq*.

IV

As we have seen in the foregoing section, creation is primarily and essentially a temporal event. It is a temporal event in that it consists in something being transposed from the state of non-existence, i.e. the state of ontological impossibility, into the state of existence, i.e. the state of ontological necessity, by the activity of the Cause at a certain point of time, i.e. as soon as the ontological "condition" is actualized. We must note, however, that for Hamadání there is hidden under the conception of creation a more fundamental state of affairs which is in itself atemporal, namely God's being the ultimate source of all existent things. From this point of view, creation is nothing but a special form in which this essentially atemporal state of affairs is conceived and represented by the human mind in accordance with the rules of the "domain of reason." In other words, imagination cannot represent, the intellect cannot conceive of, God's being the ultimate ground of existence for everything except in the form of a temporal event, called "creation."

In the "domain beyond reason," however, God's being the ultimate metaphysical ground assumes an entirely different form. The most important key-term here is "God's Face" (*wajh allāh*). What corresponds to "creation" is expressed on this level of discourse by "God's Face." This phrase, which has its immediate origin in the Qur'an, is philosophically used by Hamadání as a symbolic expression for a very peculiar relation holding between the ultimate Ground of existence and all existent things. The relation is to be conceived as absolutely preclusive of all associations with the notion of time. It is a timeless, metaphysical relation (*nisba*).

The Qur'an in more than one place makes reference to God's Face. One of the key-passages is the following:

> To God belong both the East and the West. So wheresoever you may turn, there is God's Face (Surah 11:115).

Thus God's Face is everywhere. He turns his Face to everything. And everything exists by His turning His Face toward it. All things are sustained in existence by being directly exposed to the existence-providing light which emanates from God's Face. At the first glance it might look as if we had here a very simple and ordinary kind of dyadic relation between God and the world: (x R y) which would read "God faces the world" with its converse (y R x) reading "The world faces God"—in short, a perfectly symmetrical relation. And in fact Hamadání sometimes does use in reference to this relation the word *muqábala* meaning literally "mutual facing."

The expression, however, is simply misleading, for the relation as Hamadání conceives it is a peculiar instance of an asymmetrical relation usually exemplified by "father of," "greater than." etc. The elucidation of this point will lead us into the very core of Hamadání's metaphysics on the trans-rational level of discourse.

The basic relation (x R y) reading "God faces the world" does not, in Hamadání's understanding, simply mean that x and y stand face to face in the general context of existence. It is to be taken as indicating that there is an existential energy (which Hamadání calls the "light of existence") issuing forth from x and proceedings towards y. But since there is no time in the dimension of which we are talking now, the existential energy has in reality no time to "proceed." Rather, the existential energy being activated, all existent things are actualized on the spot, there and then. The things are but so many instantaneous crystallizations of the existential energy. God's Face does not precede the world in terms of time; its precedence is conceivable only in terms of ontological rank (*rutba*).[22]

It is noteworthy that in theological terminology the basic relation (x R y) reads "God *knows* everything," for God's turning His Face toward something means nothing other than God's knowing it. And God's knowing it means in the terminology of Hamadání that the thing exists.[23]

The nature of the basic relation (x R y) being such, it will immediately be noticed that it does not allow of being simply converted to (y R x). God faces the world, but the world has no face to turn toward God. For everything in the world is in itself and by itself a sheer "nothing."[24] We can even go a step further and say that "where there is God there absolutely is nothing." This last statement is primarily a reference to what mystics actually see in the state of self-annihilation (*fanā'*) in which all things without a single exception are seen to be absorbed and dissolved into the absolute unity of existence which, alone remains in its dazzling splendor. Says the Qur'an:

> All that exists upon the earth perishes and disappears; there still abides the Face of your Lord in His majestic splendor (Surah 55:26-27).

> All things are perishable except His Face (Surah 28:88).

The conception, however, has also an ontological significance, in the sense that it indicates that everything which *seems* to exist is in reality non-existent. Paradoxically though it may sound, every "existent" (*mawjūd*) is essentially "non-existent" (*ma'dūm*). Says Hamadānī "Everything, in so far as it is considered in itself, i.e. apart from the sustaining power of God, is non-existent."[25] But—another paradox—this non-existent thing is existent in so far as it is considered in relation to God's Face.[26] "Every existent thing, except God, has no reality (*dhāt*) of its own; thus it has no existence. Its being existent has no real ground except in so far as it is contiguous to the eternal Reality."[27] Mystically this is a reference to the state of "survival" (*baqā'*). Ontologically it means the denial of the self-subsistence of things together with the assertion of their real existence as reflections of Existence. Theologically it means that everything exists in so far as it is known by God.

Thus, to come back to the point from which we started, the converse of our original relation (*x* R *y*), i.e. (*y* R *x*), can only read: *y* has "a certain relation (*nisba ma*)" to *x*.[28] That is to say, all things stand in a certain relation to God's Face, and if it were not for this relation nothing in the world would exist. But this "certain relation" cannot surely be "facing."

The relation in question is really a very peculiar one. For (y R x) is not a relation obtaining between two solidly established entities. As we have just seen, y is essentially a non-thing, while x, being God, is something infinite. It is a relation subsisting between a non-thing and an infinite thing. But the existence of such a relation is equivalent to its non-existence. "All existent things altogether have no relation at all to the infinite width of Divine Knowledge."[29] All things put together, Hamadání says, are but a single atom (*dharrah*) in the presence of Divine Knowledge. And to this he adds: "Nay, even an atom is still *something* at least; in reality the whole of all existent things is *nothing* in relation to Divine Knowledge."[30]

Since, in this way, y is essentially a non-thing, i.e. nothing, and x is infinite, the distance separating one from the other is infinite. That is to say, seen from the point of view of y, x is infinitely remote and removed from the latter so that there can actually be no relation to be established between the two terms except the negative relation of non-relation, for the two terms here can in no wise be positively connected with one another.

Since, however, the original relation (x R y) does obtain—and seen in terms of this formulation, x, instead of being infinitely remote from y, is infinitely close to it—we cannot say that (y R x) is sheer nothing either. Hence the very peculiar nature of the relation (y R x): it is and it is not at one and the same time.

It is this unusual metaphysical situation that Hamadání refers to when he says: "Every thing is present to (*hádir li*) God, whereas God is present with (*hádir ma'a*) every thing."[31] This small particle "with" (*ma'a*) is one of the key technical terms of Hamadání. He refers to the idea also in abstract form, *ma'íyah* (literally "withness"). The point is that God is "with" every single thing, but not even a single thing is "with" God. It is inconceivable, he says, "that anything whatsoever could ever exist 'with' God, because nothing possesses the rank of 'with-ness' vis-á-vis His existence. Thus it is not for anything to be 'with' God, but He is 'with' everything. If it were not for His 'with-ness' nothing indeed would remain in existence."[32] The most important part of what is indicated by this statement is the idea that a thing—corresponding to y in our formula (y R x)—does not and can not exist 'with' God(x) as something facing God, as something self-subsistent and separate from Him, and this even when it is empirically or physically existent. How can this be otherwise when the basic relation (x R y) itself is an exclusive product of x? The relation is realized not because there are two terms x and y. The very term y is a product of x's "with-ness." Y maintains its essentially precarious existence only in so far as God is "with" it as indicated by the relation (x R y). But if we view this relation starting from y taken as something existent—as suggested by the outward form of the converse of the relation, i.e. (y R x)— we find y, to our surprise, deprived of all ontological solidity, somewhat in the nature of a shadow, a reflected image in the mirror."[33] It is this lack of ontological solidity that makes y unable to be "with" x.

Another significant fact about the relation (y R x), according to Hamadání, is its timelessness. That is to say, all things in relation to God's Face are equidistant in terms of time, there being no distinction here between the past, present, and future. A thing happened yesterday; another thing happens today; still another will happen tomorrow. All the three things stand in exactly the same relation to God. "The relation of all existents to God is one. Those that exist at present, those that existed in the past, and those that will exist in the future

135

are equal to each other in their relation to God. It is our reason that establishes temporal succession among them, thinking that *this* precedes *that*."[34] The timelessness of the relation here in question is ultimately due to the fact which we have observed earlier, namely, that for Hamadání all things are essentially non-things. They simply do not exist in the strict sense in the "domain beyond reason."

Time, as it were, is the locus of motion (*zarf al-haraka*), and motion is actualized only where there are bodies."[35] Thus where there are only non-things, i.e. where there is nothing, time cannot be actualized. In other words, in the domain (which is accessible only to mystics) in which nothing "other" than God exists, the actualization of a time-order is entirely out of question. Says Hamadání: "Absolutely no self-subsistent thing exists in the domain where the Absolute exists, neither at present nor in the past nor again in the future. He who maintains that the world is now existent 'with' the existence of the Absolute is making a grave mistake, For in the domain in which the Absolute is, there is neither space nor time."[36]

The timelessness of the "domain beyond reason" brings Hamadání to the problem of eternity. Eternity is for him nothing other than this timelessness transposed forcefully, as it were, to the temporal order of things and expressed in terms of time. Now in the intellectual tradition of Islam two basic kinds of eternity are distinguished: one is "pre-eternity" (*azaliyya*) and the other is "post-eternity" (*abadiyya*). "Pre-eternity" is visioned in the direction of the past; it is the beginningless past. When one does not reach any starting-point for the existence of a thing, no matter how far back one may trace it in the past, one calls it "pre-eternal" (*azalí*). It goes without saying that in the Islamic context of thought God is the only existent that is entitled to be qualified by this

CREATION AND THE TIMELESS ORDER OF THINGS

adjective. "Post-eternity" is the opposite of "pre-eternity." It means that a thing does not reach any end in the direction of the future. Here again God is the only existent that can properly be called "post-eternal" (*abadî*). All this is perfectly correct as long as we remain consciously in the "domain of reason" and philosophize on that level. But it would be a gross mistake to think that this is the final and ultimate truth of the matter. From the point of view of the "domain beyond reason," pre-eternity is not a matter of the past; nor is post-eternity a matter of the future. For, as we have seen above, there is in this domain neither past nor future. And in such a domain pre-eternity and post-eternity must necessarily coincide with each other. We shall bring the present paper to an end by quoting an interesting passage in which Hamadání discusses this problem in a way which is very typical of him.

> He who thinks that pre-eternity is something to be sought for in the direction of the past is making an inexcusable mistake. But this is a mistake committed by the majority of the people. I say it is a mistake, because in the domain in which pre-eternity is really actualized there is neither past nor future. Pre-eternity covers the future time as well as the past time without any distinction between them. Those who cannot help imagining between them a distinction are simply compelled to do so because their reason is still in the shackles of their habit of relying upon visual imagination.
>
> In reality, the time of Adam is just as close to us as this present time of ours. For in the presence of pre-eternity to different times turn out to the one and the same. Perhaps the relation of pre-eternity to different times may best be compared to the relation of knowledge to various places. In fact, the knowledge (of various things) are not differentiated from one another in terms of being close to a place or being far from a place.[37] Rather knowledge bears one and the same

relation to all places. Knowledge is 'with' every place, whereas no place is 'with' knowledge.

Exactly in the same way must one conceive of the relation which pre-eternity bears to time. For not only is pre-eternity 'with' every unit of time and 'in' every unit of time, but it comprehends in itself every unit of time and precedes every unit of time in existence, whereas time cannot comprehend pre-eternity just as no place can comprehend knowledge.

Once you have understood what I have just said, it will be easier for you to understand that there is no distinction at all between pre-eternity and post-eternity in terms of their reality. But when this same reality is considered as a related to the past, it is provisionally called pre-eternity, while when it is considered as related to the future it is called post-eternity. These two different words are needed simply because of the two different relations.[38]

In connection with the problem of creation there is another interesting thesis Hamadání puts forward in *Zubdat al-haqá'iq*, namely, the concept of continuous creation, corresponding to the "perpetual creation (*khalq jadíd*) of Ibn 'Arabí. We will explore this issue in the following chapter.

NOTES

1. 'Ayn al-Qudát (1093-1131 C.E.), Suhrawardí al-Maqtúl (1153-1191 C.E.), Ibn 'Arabí (1165-1240 C.E.).

2. On the nature of hikmat philosophy in Iran, see my *The Concept and Reality of Existence* (Tokyo: Keio Institute of Cultural and Linguistic Studies, 1971), 57-149 and Henry Corbin, *En Islam iranien: Aspects spirituels et philosophique* 4 vols. (Paris: Gallimard, 1972).

3. In the interests of brevity and uniformity, I shall draw in this essay exclusively on his major philosophic work *Zubdat al-haqá'iq*

(Arabic), which has been edited and published by Dr. Afif Osseiran as a volume in the publications of Teheran University (No. 695), 1962.

4. That is, as long as he tries to expound his ideas philosophically in a rational way. Sometimes he talks purely as a mystic, as he does in his *Tamhídát* (Persian) edited by Afif Osseiran, Teheran, 1962. In these mystical writings he shows quite a different pattern of thinking.

5. For lack of space I cannot here go into details about what Hamadání wrote in regards to the essential function of reason. For this particular problem see *Zubdat al-haqá'iq*, XV, 25; XVII, 27; XVIII, 28; XLIII, 48; XCVII, 98.

6. Ibid., XCI, 92; LVII, 63.

7. Ibid., XI, 27. "The domain beyond reason" is one of the most important key-concepts of Hamadání. It is designated by a number of different phrases (see I, 10; XIV, 23; XXIV, 32; XXVIII, 36). Sometimes Hamadání uses the plural *atwár* "domains" or "regions" to indicate the existence of gradation in this domain (see XVI, 27; XCV, 96; XCVI, 97).

8. Ibid., XXVII, 35.

9. Ibid., XI, 26-27.

10. See the previous chapter for a discussion of this aspect of the linguistic problem of mystical philosophy according to Hamadání.

11. *Zubdat al-haqá'iq*, II, 12.

12. Ibid., VII, 17.

13. Ibid., III, 13. See also IV, 14; V, 15.

14. Ibid., XXXI, 38; XXXII, 39.

15. Ibid., VIII, 18.

16. Ibid., XXXVII, 43-44.

17. Ibid., XLVII, 52.

18. Ibid., XLVII, 53.

19. Ibid., I, 10. Reading *má lá wujúd shurúti-hi* instead of *má yajib.*

20. Ibid., I, 10 and XLVIII, 53-54.

21. Ibid., XXXVII, 43-44; XLI, 47.

22. Ibid., XLIV, 49.

23. Ibid., X, 20. On the problem of God's knowledge according to Hamadání, see chapter 4 of this book pages 109-117.

24. *Zubdat al-haqá'iq.*, LII, 56.

25. Ibid., XXXI, 38.

26. Ibid.

27. Ibid., XXXVIII, 44.

28. Ibid., XV, 27.

29. Ibid., XV, 25. As pointed out above, "divine Knowledge" is but a theological expression for the ultimate source of existence.

30. Ibid., XLV, 50.

31. Ibid., XII, 21.

32. Ibid., LVII, 62-63.

33. Ibid., XLII, 47.

34. Ibid., XV, 23-24.

35. Ibid., L, 54-55.

36. Ibid., LII. Thus Hamadání eliminates both space and time from the "domain beyond reason." And this is not the only place he does so. In fact, he repeatedly reminds us that the domain lies beyond time and space, that it is timeless and spaceless. In practice, however, when it comes to describing the structure of this domain he usually has recourse to spatial concepts and images. Or we may more positively say that Hamadání—at least in his verbal presentation—tends to reduce everything in this domain to spatial relations. Is this due to the very nature of his original visions? Or is it rather merely a matter of linguistic description? This could be a very interesting, but also very controversial question.

37. Hamadání means to say that the essential structure of knowledge *qua* knowledge does not change whether the object known happens to be far away or near. The knowledge of a star far off in the sky does not differ in this respect from the knowledge of this table here in this room.

38. Ibid., LIV, 59.

CHAPTER 6

THE CONCEPT OF PERPETUAL CREATION IN ISLAMIC MYSTICSM AND ZEN BUDDHISM

THE MAIN PROBLEM to be discussed in this essay[1] is the structure of the concept of "perpetual creation" that has developed among the Sufi thinkers around the Qur'ánic expression *khalq jadíd*, meaning literally "a new creation."

The expression is found in the Qur'án (Surah 50: 15): *Bal hum fí labsin min khalqin jadíd* ("Nay, they are in utter bewilderment regarding a new creation").

Needless to say, "new creation" in this context is a reference to the resurrection of the bodies on the Day of Judgment. The disbelievers are "in utter bewilderment" because they find it hard to believe that the bones and ashes into which they will have turned after death should be re-created anew into the original human form. Such, in brief, is the literal, or "exoteric" (*záhirí*) meaning of the *khalq jadíd* in the Qur'ánic context.

In *hikmat* philosophy, however, the same expression is given an entirely different interpretation—the so-called "internal" or "esoteric" (*bátiní*) interpretation—in the light of which the "new creation" acquires quite a new meaning; it becomes a totally different concept indicating a certain important aspect of mystical experience or mystical awareness. It is this particular, *hikmat* meaning of "new creation" that I should like to analyze in this paper. As will be made clear presently, the Qur'ánic expression *khalq jadíd,* in the kind of esoteric context we are interested in, is more properly to be translated as "ever-new creation" (rather than "new creation"), or "perpetual creation."

But instead of going further and starting immediately to analyze the idea of "perpetual creation" as understood by the mystic philosophers of Islam, I should like to discuss first a similar idea—a perfectly parallel case, we should say—that is observable in Zen Buddhism in Japan, notably in the metaphysical thought of one of its most outstanding representatives, Master Dôgen. I would take this roundabout course not only by way of writing an essay in comparative philosophy, but also, and primarily, in order to show through a concrete example (1) the universal existence of the idea of "perpetual creation" in mysticism, no matter to which historical religion it may belong; and (2) the fact that in such a context the "perpetual creation," far from being a product of philosophical thinking, or an intellectual construct, is a living vision, an experiential idea directly reflecting one of the crucial aspects of mystical awareness.

II

Dôgen (1200–1253 C.E.), whom I have chosen in this paper as the representative of Japanese Zen, is an outstanding figure in the history of Zen Buddhism. A Zen master of the Kamakura Period (1185–1333 C.E.), he is known for the depth of his spiritual experience no less than for his remarkable ability— he was in fact unprecedented in this respect—of philosophical thinking and, in particular, of expressing his thought in Japanese prose. Unlike the majority of Zen masters, whether Chinese or Japanese, who take a determined stand against all thinking, not to speak of philosophizing, Dôgen undauntedly puts what he has realized in pure meditation into the mold of consistently developed thinking, so that in reading his writings we are made to witness the intimacy of his Zen experience as it gradually unfolds itself in the form of an inner speech, although, to be sure, his "logic" or his pattern of thinking is so peculiar and original that one would hesitate to call it "philosophizing" in the ordinary sense of the term. However it may be, the result of this peculiar thinking has come down to us in a voluminous work entitled *Shôbô Genzô* ("The Quintessence of the Righteous View of Reality").

Let us now turn directly to a celebrated passage in this book, in which Dôgen explains in his own way an idea which would correspond to the idea of "perpetual creation" in Islamic mysticism. In order to convey the "feel" of his style I shall first reproduce the passage in a literal translation, and then explain what he really means to say.

> Firewood turns into ashes. The ashes can never go backward and regain the form of firewood. On the basis of the observation of this fact, however, one should not hastily conclude that the ashes are posterior and the firewood prior.
>
> Know that firewood remains established in its own *dharma*-position (i.e. its ontological position) of "being firewood;" yet, in this position, it has "before" and "after."

Although it has "before" and "after," it is cut off from "before" and "after." Ashes, likewise, remain in the *dharma*-position of "being-ashes," yet, in this position, they have "before" and "after."[2]

This text may be explicated in the following way. Imagine firewood burning into ashes. Observing what happens in this case, most people will naturally think that what was at first wood has become, i.e. has been transformed into, ashes. A certain substance, in other words, contines to exist throughout the whole process, and at a certain point of time changes its form and becomes something else. This, Dôgen points out, is nothing but a misconception based on the illusory appearance of reality. Wood can never *become* ashes. It simply appears to become ashes. Wood is ontologically immovable from its "being-wood." Wood is wood, nothing else. Yet, even while the burning wood in our example was still wood, it was not really one and the same piece of wood continuing to exist over a certain span of time before it was transformed into ashes. For, even in the *dharma*-position of being-wood, it had at every moment "before" and "after." That is to say, even under the seemingly same form of wood, there was in reality a series of instantaneous forms of wood, each coming into existence at this moment and going into non-existence the very next moment.

All this would seem to indicate clearly that from the point of view of Dôgen, the ordinary view concerning wood—for example, that it is a substance, a self-subsistent entity that continues to exist in its ontological fixity until it turns into something else—is nothing but an illusion. Surely, he says at the outset that "firewood turns into ashes . . . ." But this is a reference to the illusory appearance of things as seen through the eyes of the man in the street. Then: "firewood remains in its ontological position of being-firewood." This again is a kind of concession to the common-sense view. It can at most be nothing other than a reference to the way things are ordinarily named. For at every instant what is called (and regarded as) firewood is somethingh absolutely new, having nothing to do with what it was an instant before and what it will be an instant after.

Commenting upon this passage a Zen master of our own days, Hakuun Yasutani makes the following interesting remark.[3] Referring to the above-quoted statement of Dôgen ["Firewood remains established in its ontological position, and, while remaining established in its ontological position, it has *before* and *after*. Although it has *before* and *after*, it is cut off from *before* and *after*"] Yasutani says that these words must not be taken in their surface meaning, because Master Dôgen presents here his thought in a form that would accord with the ordinary thinking-pattern of ordinary people. What he really means to say, Yasutani continues, is that "firewood is not firewood; firewood has absolutely no time to remain established in its ontological position; it has neither *before* nor *after*; it is cut off from both *before* and *after*."

This is so because firewood is in itself almost a non-existent, having no self-subsistent reality of its own. Or, we might say, it has only an instantaneous reality. In any case, its ontological status is so insecure that it cannot continue to exist even for two moments. Everything is, at every instant, "cut off from *before* and *after*." That is to say, every single thing, taken as an ontological whole and viewed as a continuously existent entity, is in reality nothing but a series of momentary existents or a series of ontological moments. Everything is thus coming into existence to be annihilated instantaneously and then to come into existence again. The whole world is born afresh at every moment.

Considered as a philosophical thesis, the idea of the momentariness of existence would rather seem to be commonplace, particularly in Buddhism for which "ephemerality" has from the very beginning been regarded as one of its fundamental ideas. What makes the above-quoted passage—there are many other similar passages in his book—particularly important for our present purposes is the fact that Dôgen here is describing something which he has actually witnessed and experienced. It is a personal testimony of Dôgen, not a philosophic thesis. Far from being a product of rational thinking in the nature of a scholastic atomism, these are evidently words that well up from the depths of his own spiritual awareness. What he is trying to convey is is own vision of reality as he has seen it in the state of contemplation. This is why the momentariness of existence is not for him "ephemerality" in a purely negative sense, i.e. something grievous and tragic. Quite the contrary, ephemerality in the vision of a Dôgen is something positive, soothing, and even invigorating, for it *is* the true picture of the reality of existence. This point will be made more clear in what follows.

In another place in the book, Dôgen talks of the "walking of the mountain." This is in reference to the famous dictum of Master Kai (1042–1117 C.E.) of the Tai Yô Mountain: "The green mountain is constantly walking." "Mountain" is mentioned here as a symbol of immobility, for mountains appears to the eyes of the ordinary man to be solidly and firmly established, eternally immovable. In the light of what we have been above, however, the "green mountain" is not at all immobile; on the contrary, it is constantly moving in the sense that it appears and disappears moment by moment. And precisely in this process of incessant appearing-disappearing Dôgen witnesses the actualization *hic et nunc* of the timeless (or super-temporal) dimension of reality. Says Dôgen:

The mountain is perfect and complete in its being-mountain. Therefore it is timelessly at peace (in being a mountain) and constantly walking. You should never doubt the walking of the mountain, for the walking of the mountain is essentially similar to the walking of a man, no matter how different its movement may appear on the surface from the way man walks by the movement of his legs.

Just because of its constant walking, the mountain continues to be a mountain. Indeed, the walking of the mountain is more brisk and rapid than a gust of stormy wind. But those who exist in the mountain are not aware of it. "In-the-mountain" refers to the exuberant florescence of Being within the world.

Nor are those who exist outside the mountain aware of its walking. It is but natural that those who have no eye to see (the reality of) the mountain should be unaware of the Truth; they simply do not know It, do not see It, do not hear It.

The expression: "Water flows" does not shock anyone. Everybody thinks it quite natural that water flows. But Dôgen remarks, ordinary people do not in truth know the real meaning of the expression "water flows." Their ignorance is immediately disclosed by the very fact that they are invariably shocked when they hear someone say: "Mountains flow." For "a flowing mountain" and "flowing water" refer exactly to the same aspect of reality. Here Dôgen quotes from the "Record of Sayings and Doings" of Master Un Mon (Chinese: Yün Mên, 864–949 C.E.):

> Once a monk asked Un Mon: "What is the ultimate birth-place of all Buddhas?"
> "The Eastern Mountain goes flowing on the water."

The question: "What is the ultimate birth-place of all Buddhas?" means "How is in your view the ultimate Reality?" To this

Un Mon gave a seemingly irrelevant answer, pointing to the "flowing of the mountain." He could as well said: "The mountain does *not* flow," just as he could have said: "Water does not flow." For in truth, Dôgen says, the ultimate, absolute reality of the mountain does flow in a certain respect (i.e. in view of its being-mountain through a series of successive ontological instants), and does *not* flow in another respect (i.e. in view of the actualization of Eternity in the very succession of ontological instants).

The argument here developed by Dôgen is based on a very original idea of his concerning the relation between time and existence. Existence, for Dôgen, is but a moment's flash. Everything, as we have seen above, goes on being renewed moment by moment. At every moment existence is absolutely new; it is "cut off from *before* and *after*."

For a right understanding of what Dôgen says concerning this problem, it is of utmost importance that we never lose sight of the fact that for him time is completely identical with existence.[5] In his view, time is not a sort of locus in which things exist and events occur; nor is it an innate form of human cognition. Rather, time *is* existence itself. And, we must remember, time is essentially an instant. Thus to say: "Such-and-such a thing exists at this instant" is exactly the same as saying: "this instant!" In other words, the former expression implies a tautology. For "this instant" by itself means the ontological moment, i.e. the momentary existence of this particular thing; the annihilation of "this-instant" is the annihilation of "this-thing," and *vice versa*.

On the other hand, however, in each one of these ontological instants Dôgen witnesses the actualization of what he calls *nikon,* the closest translation of which will probably be the "timeless Now," meaning Timelessness or Eternity as it crystallizes itself in "this-instant." Time here is the actualization of Timelessness. And viewed from the vantage point of this position, all the separate instant-things disclose their fundamental unity in the sense that they are seen existing all simultaneously in a metaphysical dimension beyond time. This point is explained by Dôgen himself in the following way.[6]

Suppose I saw something (say, X) yesterday. And suppose I see something else (say, Y) today. Since "yesterday" and "today" are different and separated from one another in terms of time, X which I saw yesterday cannot be the same as Y which I see today. X is no longer here, while Y is still with me, within my ken. But from the point of view of the "timeless Now," the distinction between "yesterday" and "today" totally disappears, and consequently the distinction between X and Y. Says Dôgen: I go deep into a mountainous region, reach the peak of the highest mountain, and, standing there, look over the thousands of peaks that lie under my feet. All the peaks are there, clearly visible, all together, simultaneously. An unlimited expanse of mountain ranges is within a sweep of the eye. The particular mountain (X) which I saw yesterday is there just as the mountain (Y) which I saw today. There is no distinction here between "yesterday" and "today." The mountain (X) which I saw yesterday is still with me in my "timeless Now." For nothing passes away in this dimension.

The pine-tree, Dôgen goes on to argue, has the time (i.e. the series of instants) of its being-pine. But it is also my "timeless Now."[7] The bamboo has the time of its being-bamboo, and it is different from the time of the pine. Yet, it is also my "timeless Now." And in being my "timeless Now," the time of the pine is identical with the time of the bamboo. That is to say, the pine and the bamboo—indeed all other things too— are simultaneously present in the eternal Now.

Thus concludes Dôgen, the world, if considered from the point of view of time, will appear as an interminable succession of temporal units, whether long or short. But—and this is the important point—in each of these temporal units, whether taken as long (as an hour, day, month, year, etc.) or short (as a moment, an instant, a fraction of a second, etc.), all the remaining units of time are actualized. In other words, each single unit of time is an actualization of the whole of time. And since, as we have pointed out earlier, a unit of time, for Dôgen, is completely identical with a unit of existence, the above-statement means nothing other than that each single thing at each of its successive ontological moments is an actualization of the All.

Now to summarize Dôgen's thought in so far as it has a direct bearing upon our problem, "perpetual creation." Time *is* being. Thus a unit of time is a unit of existence. The shortest fraction of time, an instant, is therefore to be considered an ontological instant. Every "thing" so called is nothing but a series of such ontological instants. Nothing in this sense remains existent even for two moments. At every moment the "thing" is new. A thing at this moment, for instance, is completely "cut off" from what it was a moment ago and from what it will be a moment later.

There is, on the other hand, a totally different dimension of time-being, which is always to be actually experienced in the practice of Zen contemplation as *my* "timeless Now." In this dimension, all things are viewed simultaneously, all differences between them in terms of time having been completely obliterated. For each single ontological instant is here an actualization of all other ontological instants.

Understood in this way, Dôgen's concept of time = timelessness will find an Islamic counterpart in the thought of 'Ayn al-Qudát al-Hamadání, which we are going to discuss in the following section.

III

Leaving Zen Buddhism at this point and turning now to the mystical philosophy of Islam ('irfán),[8] I would propose to take up first 'Ayn al-Qudát al-Hamadání, 1098–1131 C.E.) as its representative. Hamadání in fact was a remarkable thinker who played an exceedingly important role in the formative process of Islamic mystical philosophy at its earliest historical phase. In many respects he is rightly to be considered an immediate forerunner of the *Magister Maximus*, Ibn 'Arabí (1165–1240 C.E.). It must be remembered that he was a direct disciple of the great mystic Ahmad al-Gházálí and an indirect disciple of Ahmad's brother, the celebrated Muhammad al-Ghazálí (known in the West in the Middle Ages as Algazel). From the latter he acquired an intellectual training of the highest refinement, including philosophy and theology, plus an initiation into the atmosphere of mysticism. By the hand of the former he was brought right into the very core of Islamic mysticism and its esoteric teaching. By dint of this happy combination of a rigorous training in rational thinking and a most personal kind of discipline in mystical practice could Hamadání become quite an original thinker deserving to be considered one of the most important precursors of the long Iranian tradition of *hikmat* philosophy.

In trying to elucidate the idea of "perpetual creation" in Hamadání, we must start from his distinction between (1) "the domain (or dimension) of reason"[9] (*tawr al-'aql*) and (2) "the domain (or dimension) beyond reason (*tawr wará'a al-'aql*), for this distinction is the highest and most fundamental principle underlying the whole architecture of his thinking. Whatever problem we may take up, we are, in the case of Hamadání, always and necessarily brought back to this highest principle. Without having recourse to this distinction between the two domains, none of the key concepts of Hamadání can properly be elucidated.[10]

It is to be noted at the outset that each of these two domains must be understood as (a) a subjective state of consciousness and (b) an objective state of reality, although Hamadání, when he writes, does not distinguish between (a) and (b), and uses the terms "domain of reason" and "domain beyond reason" without clarifying whether the reference is to (a) or (b). In a certain sense he is quite justified in doing so because as a mystic he does not see any real distinction between subject and object, and because, in a world where a subjective state of consciousness is in itself an objective state of reality, there can be no discrepancy between epistemology and metaphysics.

The "domain of reason" as an inner state of the subject means the rational, analytic function of reason which is exercised on the basis of materials furnished by sense experience. Objectively it means the empirical world, the phenomenal dimension of reality, in which reason fulfills its natural role.

As to the "domain beyond reason" which, as one could imagine, occupies the key position in Hamadání's system, it means when taken in the (a) sense—and in this sense it is often called by Hamadání *núr fí al-bátin*, "interior light"—the deepest layer of consciousness, in which the human mind, losing its own purely "human" character, comes into direct contact with the "divine" order of things. Understood in the (b) sense, it refers to the "divine" order of things, i.e. the trans-rational and supra-sensible dimension of reality, which will disclose itself only to the awareness of a mystic in deep contemplation.

Of course, the distinction itself between the two "domains" has nothing particular and characteristic about it. Rather, it is very commonplace, or perhaps too commonplace even to be mentioned. For the very conception of a mystic confined to the domain of reason and sensation is simply absurd. What makes this distinction really original in the case of Hamadání is the fact that each of the major concepts of Islamic theology is consistently and systematically given a double interpretation in terms of the distinction between the "domain of reason" and the "domain beyond reason," so much so that one and the same idea usually appears in Hamadání's thought in two entirely different forms in accordance with the two different points of reference.

It goes without saying that "creation" (*khalq*) is one of the most important concepts in Islamic thought. But "creation," it is important to notice, is in the system of Hamadání a matter properly belonging to the "domain of reaon." The idea of the temporal creation of the world by God as it is ordinarily understood by the common believers as well as by the theologians cannot, from the point of view of Hamadání, but lose it validity in the "domain beyond reason." Thus Hamadání looks for a more fundamental idea that could serve as the basis for both the theological and the truly gnostic (*'irfání*) understanding of "creation." He finds it in the idea of the Absolute (or God) being the ultimate Source of existence, the ultimate Origin from which all existents derive their existence. He calls it *yanbú'-e wujúd*, "fountainhead of existence."[11]

That the Absolute is the ultimate Source of all existents means in reference to the "domain of reason" that the world is a product of the Divine act of creation. The concept of creation naturally involves the concept of time. The created world, i.e. the pheneomenal or empirical world, subsists essentially in the dimension of time. Everything here occurs in time. Everything has an ontological beginning and an ontological end.

The same *yanbú'-e wujúd*, that is, the same idea of the Absolute's being the ultimate Source of all existents, appears in the "domain beyond reason" in an entirely different form from the idea of "creation" as ordinarily understood. This is due to the fact that the "domain beyond reason" is a metaphysical region where there is, or there can be, no temporal order between things and where everything is divested of its temporal nature. It is the domain of the supra-temporal, a-temporal, order of things—a limitless and timeless expanse of existence. There is in such a region no room for any idea of creation that would in any sense involve the concept of time. There is no place here even for the *waqt mawhúm*, "imaginary time," which the philosophers and theologians talk about in reference to the essentially timeless state of affairs *before* God created the world. As a matter of fact we often use expressions like "before the creation of the world" and "after the creation of the world." According to Hamadání, such expressions make no sense in the "domain beyond reason." Where there is no time, "before" and "after" are meaningless.

In reference to this timeless dimension, the Absolute's being the ultimate Source of all existents simply means, in the view of Hamadání, that God is "with" (*ma'a*) all things. As noted in the previous chapter, this idea which he calls *ma'íyat Alláh,* "withness of God," constitutes one of the cardinal points of Hamadání's metaphysical system. He has another important technical term for exactly the same idea; namely, *wajh alláh,* "God's Face." God turns his Face—or more literally, *has* his Face—toward all things; and that precisely *is* the existence of all things.[12]

However, even in reference to the "dimension of reason (and sensation)," there are certain important respects in which Hamadání's understanding of God's temporal creation of the world radically differs from the ordinary conception of creation. Here we shall confine ourselves to discussing the particular aspect of the problem which directly concerns the idea of "perpetual creation."

The most characteristic feature of the "domain beyond reason" is for Hamadání that it is timeless and beyond time. There is no temporal evolvement; there is neither beginning nor end for anything. Nor is there any temporal succession between things; it is absurd to speak of something being prior or posterior to something else. In this dimension beyond time, Hamadání says, all things are characterized by an existential equidistance from God, the ultimate Source of existence. God is "with" all things, that is, all things in this dimension maintain exactly the same ontological distance from God. All things are thus contemplated at this stage as co-existing in a timeless expanse of existence, just like the hundreds and thousands of mountains which Dôgen says are visible all together simultaneously to the eyes of a man looking over them from the peak of the highest mountain. Yet, before the man had reached such a vantage point today, that is, when he was still wandering about in the mountainous district, climbing the mountains up and down one after another, only the tiniest portion of the district, perhaps a single mountain at the most, had been in his ken. Besides, the landscape had been changing for him from moment to moment; this because at every moment he stood in a peculiar and unique relation to the whole of the landscape.

This simile is exactly applicable to the metaphysical situation of all existents as Hamadání envisions it. For in the view of Hamadání, too, the things that co-exist all together in the "domain beyond reason" in a timeless expanse of existence, eternally still and motionless, suddenly begin to appear in a state of perpetual flux, the moment we transfer or project their figures onto the screen of the "domain of reason (and sensation)." In this dimension of temporal evolvement and succession, all things are seen constantly and incessantly moving and changing. This is, according to Hamadání, due to the fact that in the ontological dimension over which Time reigns, the relation (*nisbah*) of each one of the things to the Source of its existence is constantly changing. At every moment the relation is different from that at other moments. One and the same ontological relation never lasts even for two successive moments. And this immediately implies for Hamadání that each one of the things goes on receiving a new existence at every moment.

Hamadání explains this situation by comparing it to the way the earth becomes illumined by the light of the sun:

> The illumination of the earth by the light of the sun is possible only on the basis of a particular relation being actualized between the earth and the sun. If the relation were to come to naught, the capacity itself of the earth to receive the light of the sun would instantaneously be annihilated. It is only as long as the said relation lasts between the two that the receptivity of the earth to the light of the sun remains activated.[13]

According to Hamadání, however, the continued subsistence of one and the same relation is nothing but an illusion. For at every moment a new relation is established between the earth and the sun. But since the successive relations that are established at successive moments are so similar to each other that the "feeble-minded" and the "short-sighted"—i.e. those whose view is confined to the "domain of reason (and sensation)"—naturally imagine that the light of the sun that is illuminating the earth at this moment is just the same light which illumined the earth a moment ago and the light which will illumine the earth a moment later.

The truth is, Hamadání goes on to assert, that the relation at every single moment is unique; it is peculiar to that very moment.[14] And this applies to all things without exception. That is to say, everything derives its existence from the ultimate Source of existence by dint of a relation being actualized between the two; but this ontological relation must be renewed and re-established at every moment if the thing is to continue to exist for more than one moment.

Suppose, says Hamadání, here is a stupid man who, having seen four different persons—say, Zayd, 'Amr, Khálid, and Bakr—and having observed that they are one and the same in being-human, comes to the conclusion that they are one single person. Everybody will surely laugh at his stupidity. Yet, even those who happen to be endowed with a fully developed intelligence commit a mistake of an exactly similar nature with regard to the existence of the world. And few are those who even notice the absurdity of the mistake committed.[15]

In reality, every existent (*mawjúd*) is, according to Hamadání, in itself a non-existent thing (*ma'dúm*). The illumination of a non-existent by the "light of existence" (*núr al-wujúd*) is possible only on the basis of a certain relation actualized between it and the ultimate Source of existence. And this existential relation is at every moment entirely different from those that have preceded it as well as those that will follow it. The whole world, in other words, goes on being created afresh moment by moment.

Such, in broad outline, is the view of Hamadání regarding the idea of "perpetual creation." What is worthy of notice about it is that it is a peculiar metaphysical vision born out of his own personal mystical experience, and that it must not, therefore, be confused with the atomism of the Ash'arite theologians. Though the two positions resemble each other outwardly to a considerable extent, Hamadání's thought, being an immediate presentation of a fact of mystical awareness, is qualitatively different from an atomistic philosophy based on a purely rational analysis of the mode of existence of all things. This point will become more evident when we come to Ibn 'Arabí.

In concluding the present section I would point out that the idea itself of "perpetual creation" was thus undeniably established by Hamadání, but not the technical expression: *khalq jadíd*, "(ever-) new creation." Hamadání does not use the Qur'ánic phrase in order to indicate the idea. It is Ibn 'Arabí who, giving quite an original interpretation to the Qur'ánic verse in which this particular expression occurs, establishes it as a technical term to be used as such in the subsequent development of 'irfánic philosophy.

IV

We now turn to Ibn 'Arabí, the *Magister Maximus*. With a view to bringing into marked relief the originality of his approach to the problem of "perpetual creation," we would begin by recalling that in the course of the history of Islamic thought the same basic theme has been elaborated by many thinkers in a number of different ways.

Quite apart from the atomistic philosophy of the Ash'arites, which may be mentioned as a typical case of a purely rational or non-*hikmat* treatment of the problem, we know of several interesting approaches that have been proposed within the confines of mystical philosophy after Ibn 'Arabí. The celebrated concept of *harakah jawharíyah* or "(constant) motion in *substantia*" of Mullá Sadrá may be regarded as one of the most original philosophical elaborations of the same basic idea.

But perhaps the most popular and most widely known philosophical approach to the problem—still within the boundaries of 'irfánic philosophy—consists in explaining "perpetual creation" in terms of the essential ontological possibility (*imkán dhátí*) of all things in the world, i.e. the "possibility" which constitutes the essential make-up of each of the phenomenal things. In fact, most of the textbooks or manuals of *hikmat* philosophy that have been composed by later thinkers follow this pattern of thinking. Thus, to give a concrete example out of many well-known cases, Muhammad Láhíjí (d. ca. 1506–7 C.E.) in his important commentary on the *Gulshan-e Ráz* deals with "perpetual creation" in the following way.[16]

As has just been indicated, Láhíjí approaches this problem from the viewpoint of the essential structure of the existents in the empirical world. Every existent in this world is ontologically a *mumkin* "possible," i.e. not-necessarily-existentent. And to say that every existent has *imkán* or "ontological possibility" as its very essence is to say that everything in this world embraces within itself non-existence, that everything, taken in itself and considered by itself—i.e., considered in separation from God, the ultimate Source of existence—is '*adam*, "nothing" or "non-existent." Thus by the very requirement of its own essential negativity, every existent in the world, if left alone, immediately goes toward the nullification of itself.

Everything in this way can possess only a momentary existence. For, the moment it is brought into the sphere of being, its own nature irresistibly draws it back to the sphere of nonbeing. That every existent has as its essential nature the tendency to nullify itself is precisely what is commonly meant by "ephemerality." All things are thus ephemeral. All things, so says Láhíjí, are rushing with vertiginous speed toward the abyss of non-existence. Nothing stops even a moment.

On the other hand, however, there is the constant creative activity on the part of the Absolute—the creative activity that has been called by Ibn 'Arabí *nafas rahmání*, "the breath of the Merciful,"—which goes on conferring new existence upon the things as they go on nullifying themselves. At the very convergence-point of these two factors, i.e. (1) the essential "possibility" of all things and (2) the constant effusion of the "breath of the Merciful" from the absolute metaphysical Source, *khalq jadíd*, "perpetual creation," is actualized.

The function of the "breath of the Merciful" thus consists in retaining—or more literally "chaining" (*habs kardan*)—the essentially non-existent things to existence. But the "chaining to existence" must not be taken to mean that the things are made to exist in a continuous, uninterrupted way. That is absolutely impossible because of the essential "possibility" of the things. Rather the "chaining to existence" here in question is effectuated, according to Láhíjí, in the following manner. Every existent, by the requirement of its own ontological "possibility," has to put off the clothes of existence as soon as it comes into being. But at that very moment, the "breath of the Merciful" confers upon it a new garment of existence so that the thing is made to look as if it remained existent without any interruption. But in the fraction of a second in which the thing puts off the old garment and puts on a new garment, the mystic's eye catches a fleeting glimpse of an unfathomable abyss of non-existence gaping wide under the existence of the thing. All things in this sense, so concludes Láhíjí, are at every moment in the state of "perpetual creation" (*dar har án dar khalq-e jadíd-and*), because the relation (*nisbah*) in which every "possible" existent stands to existence is at every moment new.

The typically philosophic approach to the problem of

"perpetual creation" which we have just examined can ultimately, or partially at least, be ascribed to Ibn 'Arabí. In any
case, the idea as expounded by Láhíjí has nothing discordant
with the world-view of Ibn 'Arabí. But the latter himself has
another, far more original approach of his own to the same problem, which we are going to discuss in the following section.

V

Ibn 'Arabí deals with the problem of "perpetual creation" primarily in terms of the heart (*qalb*) of the mystic. It is highly
significant in this respect that Chapter XII of the *Fusús al-
hikam* ("Bezels of Wisdom") which is devoted precisely to a
discussion of "perpetual creation," is entitled *Hikmah
Qalbíyah*, i.e. "esoteric knowledge relating to the heart."[17]

It is to be noticed first of all that the word *qalb* is in this
particular context used as a technical term. It does not refer to
the heart as a bodily organ. It means instead a spiritual organ,
an inner locus of mystical awareness—a purely spiritual dimension of the mind in which supra-sensible and
trans-rational aspects of reality are disclosed to the mystic. In
order to distinguish the "heart" as he understands it in this
context from the heart as the bodily organ, Ibn 'Arabí uses the
expression: *qalb al-'árif* meaning literally "the heart of the
gnostic," which we might, principally for the sake of conve-
nience, translate as the spiritual heart. The seemingly quite
commonplace phrase, *qalb al-'árif*, is in reality a very special
expression peculiar to Ibn 'Arabí, because by *'árif*, "gnostic,"
is meant here the *walí* at the highest stage, i.e. *insán kámil*, the
Perfect Man.

With such an understanding, Ibn 'Arabí begins by pointing out the infinite spaciousness or comprehensiveness of the
spiritual heart. In support of his view, a famous *hadíth qudsí*

(a prophetic tradition in which God Himself talks in the first person) is adduced. It reads; *Má wasi'a-ní ard-í wa-lá samá-í. Wa-wasi'a-ní qalb 'abd-í almu'min al-taqí al-naqí,* "Neither My earth nor My sky is wide enough to contain Me. But the 'heart' of my servant, believing, pious and pure, is wide enough to contain Me." According to the interpretation of Ibn 'Arabí, "My believing, pious and pure servant" means *'árif.* That is to say, the heart as the spiritual organ is, in the case of a mystic of the highest rank, endowed with an infinite comprehensiveness to such a degree that it can contain or comprehend even the Absolute.

In order to further corroborate his own view, Ibn 'Arabí quotes utterances of some of the outstanding mystics who preceded him. A saying of Abú Yazïd al-Bastámí, for instance:

> Even if the divine Throne and all that is contained therein were to be found, infinitely multiplied, in one single corner of the mystic's heart (*qalb al-'árif*), he would not be aware of it.

Translated rather freely, this utterance means: If we were to put the whole universe (with all the things that exist therein), infinitely multiplied, into the "heart" of the mystic, that infinitely vast universe would occupy only a small corner of the "heart," so small indeed that the mystic himself would not even become conscious of it.

For a right understanding of such a statement, we must recall that the *qalb* which Ibn 'Arabí is speaking of is the heart of the Perfect Man. It is, in other words, the cosmic Mind, or cosmic and universal awareness of the Perfect Man as understood by Ibn 'Arabí.

In the view of Ibn 'Arabí, the cosmic awareness of the Perfect Man is *jámi',* "all-comprehensive;" that is, it comprehends in itself all the attributes of existence (*jamí sifát al-wujud*), i.e. all things and events that were, are, and will be actualized in the world of being. And this all-comprehensiveness of the heart is nothing other than the all-comprehensiveness of the Absolute, because all the "attributes of existence" that are said to be contained in the heart are so many self-manifestations of the Absolute. It is in this sense that the "heart of the mystic" can be said to contain even the Absolute.

We must observe at this point that the word *qalb* in its *hikmat* understanding is always etymologically associated with the word *taqallub* (from the same root consonants q-l-b). *Taqallub* means constant change or transformation, something constantly turning into something else, something incessantly assuming new forms. Thus, in the light of this understanding, the *qalb* of the mystic is characterized by constant transformation. And this *taqallub* of the mystic's *qalb* exactly corresponds to the constant and incessant ontological transformation of the Absolute known as divine *tajallí*, or "self-manifestation."

In the view of Ibn 'Arabí, the Absolute, because of its excessive metaphysical plenitude, cannot but express in external forms the inner fullness of existence. Hence what is called *fayd*, "divine emanation" or "metaphysical effusion."[18]

The Absolute is here envisioned as containing within itself an infinite number of inner articulations or, we might say, ontological inclinations. In the traditional terminology of theology these ontological articulations in the Absolute are called divine names and attributes. Each of the divine attributes requires for itself externalization. Thus the Absolute, in accordance with the ontological requirement of all its Names and attributes—the divine names are ordinarily understood to be ninety-nine but in reality they are, in Ibn 'Arabí's view, infinite in number—goes on manifesting itself in an infinite number of concrete forms.

On the other hand, as we saw earlier, the cosmic heart (*qalb*) of the mystic is spacious enough to contain even the Absolute. In the light of what we have just seen, this statement would necessarily imply that the heart goes on reflecting moment by moment all the forms in which the Absolute manifests itself. And this must precisely be what is meant by the *taqallub al-qalb* "constant transformation of the heart" of the mystic.

It is to be observed that there is no limit or end to the self-manifesting activity (*tajallī*) of the Absolute, and that the heart correspondingly has no limit in its inner transformation (*taqallub*), i.e. in its ever-increasing knowledge of the Absolute.

But this is not yet the ultimate view of the metaphysical structure of Reality, for there is still here a distinction made between the *tajallī* and *taqallub*, i.e. between the self-manifestation of the Absolute and the inner transformation of the heart. The distinction implies that the mystic's heart goes on reflecting, like a spotlessly polished mirror, the endless "self-manifestations" of the Absolute. Such, according to Ibn 'Arabí, cannot be considered the ultimate picture of Reality.

In order to reach the ultimate view, we must go a step further and transcend the stage at which the heart is imagined as reflecting the infinitely varied forms of the Absolute. For in reality, the heart in such a state is no longer human awareness to be distinguished from the *divine* self-manifestation. Quite the contrary, the heart itself in its constant inner transformation *is* nothing other than the various forms of divine self-manifestation. Conversely, the incessant transformation (*taqallub*) of the Absolute is itself the constant transformation (*taqallub*) of the heart. As Ibn 'Arabí says:

The mystic's heart takes cognizance of the constant transformation (*taqallub*) of the Absolute by the heart's own transformation into various forms.[19]

Ibn 'Arabí observes in this connection that the self (*nafs*) of the mystic in a state like this is no longer his own "human" self, his self now being perfectly identical with the *huwíyah*, the "He-ness" or "He-aspect" of the Absolute. The "He-ness" of the Absolute is the Absolute in so far as it allows of being designated as "He," if not in its original absoluteness. The divine He-ness is thus the deepest metaphysical stratum of the Absolute to which we can point with precision in so far as it manifests itself in the most individual, concrete forms.

In the spiritual state of awareness which Ibn 'Arabí is talking about here, there is no longer any substantial discrepancy between the heart of the mystic and the He-ness of the Absolute. The myustic's knowing himself is his knowing the Absolute. And the inner transformation of the mystic's heart *is* nothing other than the ontological transformation of the Absolute. This, according to Ibn 'Arabí, is the right understanding of the famous dictum: *man 'arafa nafsa-hu 'arafa rabba-hu*, "He who knows his own self knows (thereby) his Lord."

The one absolute Reality goes on assuming infinitely various and variegated forms in the dimension of phenomenal appearance. And that itself is the incessant transformation (*taqallub*) of the Absolute. One should not commit the mistake of imagining that the mystic's heart in the process of inner *taqallub* goes on reflecting the incessant ontological *taqallub* of the Absolute. For "reflection" presupposes the independent subsistence of two different things standing face to face: (1) the mirror and (2) the things that are reflected therein. But the *taqallub* here in question is not something of that nature. There is no room for something reflecting something else. For the *taqallub* here is one and the same *taqallub* on both sides.

Ibn 'Arabí thus reaches his own conception of "perpetual creation." Quoting the Qur'ánic verse (*bal hum fí labsin min khalqin jadíd*) which we cited at the outset, he remarks that those who are "spiritually blind" and deprived of mystical capacity would never be able to understand the deep meaning of the expression *khalq jadíd*, "new creation." In his interpretation, which he believes is the only right one, this particular phrase refers to the fact that, seen through the eye of a true mystic, the world is "transformed with each breath" (*tabaddul al-'álam ma'a al-anfás*) i.e. moment by moment. At every single moment the whole world emerges in a new form. And to say so is, as we have just seen, exactly the same as saying that the cosmic heart of the Perfect Man goes on assuming a new form at every moment.

For Ibn 'Arabí, all this is reducible to a simple statement: divine *tajallí* or self-manifestation never ceases to be active, and moreover it never repeats itself.

In terms of "creation," the same idea can very well be expressed by saying that the world (i.e., the heart of the Perfect Man) is created afresh moment by moment. The world which we see and in which we live at this very moment is not a continuation of the world we witnessed a moment ago. Likewise the world which is coming after a moment will again be an entirely different world from the present one.

The existence of the world as a temporal continuum is in reality a series of existences each of which emerges and disappears moment by moment. Thus, between two consecutive existences there is always a break, an ontological chasm of non-existence, no matter how short and imperceptible to the ordinary eye the break may be. And what is true of the world as a whole is of course true of every existent things. This is tantamount to saying that there is no solid substance in the world. What is usually believed to be a solid substance, a stone, for example, which our common-sense view regards as continuing to exist over a more or less long span of time, is in truth a series of exactly similar stones that are created anew one after another. There is no difference in this respect between a stone and the flame of a burning lamp. Those who think that a stone is one single solid substance are, from the point of view of an Ibn 'Arabí, still in the mental stage of children—"small children" (sibyán) in relation to grownup people, i.e. mystics. Already before Ibn 'Arabí, Hamadání had made the following remark:

> Small children, observing a lamp burning continuously, would naturally think that what they see is one single flame. But the grownups know very well that it is a series of different flames appearing and disappearing moment by moment. And from the viewpoint of the mystics this must necessarily be the case with every thing in the world except God.[20]

For Ibn 'Arabí, the world is alive with a new life at every moment. In this sense, we are—or at least we are supposed to be—tasting at every moment the absolute freshness of the original creation of the world.

VI

Ibn 'Arabí's thought regarding "perpetual creation," which we have just discussed, centers round the notion of the incessant transformation of the mystic's heart. Now if we sever the idea from its mystical background and consider it as a purely philosophical thesis, it is clearly a kind of atomism. And as an upholder of atomism, Ibn ʿArabí must of necessity confront the theological atomism of the Ashʿarites, which in fact is very similar in its outward structure to that of Ibn ʿArabí.

Ibn ʿArabí himself is aware of this outward similarity, and feels obliged to criticize the Ashʿarite position from his point of view. It is interesting to observe that in doing so he comes down, so to speak, from his mystical position to the ground of rational and philosophic thinking on which stand the Ashʿarites, and tries to refute them on that same ground.

Ibn ʿArabí starts by admitting that the Ashʿarites also discovered the idea of "perpetual creation." But, he hastens to add, they did so "quite by chance and accident." Moreover, their discovery of the truth was partial, because it was limited only to some of the existents, not covering the whole of them; namely, the Ashʿarites recognized the fact of "perpetual creation" only with regard to "accidents" to the total exclusion of "substances."

As a matter of fact, the famous dictum: *inna al-ʿarad lá yabqá zamánayn,* "No accident remains in existence for two units of time," constitutes one of the basic theses of Ashʿarite philosophy. Suppose, for example, here is a red flower. The accident, i.e. the red color, is not, according to the Ashʿarites, a temporal continuum. It is not a quality which remains actualized continuously, without any break. It is, on the contrary, something that appears and disappears, and then appears and disappears—the process continues until the color ceases to be visible or changes into some other color. But by dint of visual illusion we get the impression that one and the same color exists on the surface of the flower as a temporal continuum. But it is nothing but an illusion.

Such, in brief, is the position taken by the Ashʿarites with regard to accidents. So far so good, says Ibn ʿArabí. The mistake of Ash'arism, he continues, consists in that it does not let "perpetual creation" exceed the domain of accidents. In fact, according to the Ash'arites, substances are not subject to the ontological law of momentariness. The flower as distinguished from its color, for example, is considered a solid entity which continues to subsist for many units of time. Curiously enough, however, a substance in Ash'arite ontology is nothing but a whole composed of a number of different accidents (*majmú' al-a'rád*).

The Ash'arites are certainly right, Ibn 'Arabí argues, in maintaining that no accident remains existent for more than one unit of time. On the other hand, however, they hold that a substance is a whole composed of accidents. Then, their thesis will be tantamount to saying that those elements none of which continues to exist even for two moments, do constitute, when gathered together, an entity continuing to exist over many units of time. This is, Ibn 'Arabí concludes, an absurdity even in the dimension of rational thinking.

In Ibn 'Arabí's own view, there is absolutely nothing in the world, be it a substance or an accident, remaining in existence for more than one moment. If we insist on using the philosophical terminology of "substance-accident" distinction, we shall have to maintain that whatever exists in the world is an accident. Things like tables, flowers, men, etc., are accidents just as much as are their *so-called* accidents like colors and forms.

Accidents of what, then? The question is legitimate because the very word "accident" would make no sense philosophically, if there were no substance in which accidents could inhere.

Thus, still using the same philosophical terminology, Ibn 'Arabí gives the following answer to this question. These "accidents" (e.g. tables, flowers, their colors and forms) are all accidents of the ultimate and only self-subsistent Substance which is none other than the Absolute. All existents in the world—whether so-called substances or so-called accidents—are in reality accidents that appear and disappear on the surface of the ultimate Substance, just like innumerable bubbles that appear and disappear on the surface of water. They are all "accidents" because even those things which the philosophers recognize as substances in distinction from accidents are, in the view of Ibn 'Arabí, nothing other than so many special self-determinations of the ultimate Substance. Thus, Ibn 'Arabí concludes: *inna al-'álam kulla-hu majmú a'rád,* "The world in its entirety is a whole composed of accidents."[21]

Concerning the argument which we have just examined there is a point which is of vital importance for a right understanding of Ibn 'Arabí's position on this problem. I shall bring this paper to a close by clarifying this particular point.

As we have noticed, Ibn 'Arabí regards in this context the Absolute or God as the ultimate and eternal Substance. This expression is misleading. We must not lose sight of the fact that Ibn 'Arabí is here using the Aristotelian terminology of "substance-accident" distinction in a metaphorical way. To regard God as a "substance"—no matter how special the image of that "substance" may be—is for Ibn 'Arabí nothing but a philosophical metaphor. For, in his view, God is pure existence. And being pure existence, it must be above all categorization. Furthermore, it must be remembered that even in non-mystical philosophy, the Absolute does not, strictly speaking, allow itself to be categorized as a "substance." Pure existence transcends the Aristotelian distinction between substance and accident.

But it is important to note that Ibn 'Arabí is here trying to refute the Ash'arites on their own ground. And in this sense he is fully justified in speaking of God as the Substance with all things in the world as its accidents. For this is after all simply another way of saying—which is one of his most fundamental theses—that the Absolute *quá* pure existence never ceases to diversify itself into an infinite number of concrete existents.

Thus Ibn ʿArabí's position, if considered as a purely philosophical thesis, presents a striking similarity to the Ashʿarite atomism—the only difference between the two, as I have just pointed out, being that Ibn ʿArabí does not make in this particular context any distinction whatsoever between the so-called substances and accidents, for he regards them all as "accidents" of the divine Substance, whereas the Ashʿarites ascribe the momentariness of existence here in question only to the *so-called* accidents as distinguished from substances.

But of course there is between the two camps a far more profound difference. The Ashʿarite thesis is a product of rational thinking, while Ibn ʿArabí's thesis is a philosophical elaboration of his own mystical vision of the world. This difference is clear if only for the reason that the vision of the universal, constant change of all things, i.e., the vision of "perpetual creation," is, according to Ibn ʿArabí, a supersensory vision allowed only to the cosmic heart of the Perfect Man, which is identical with the He-ness of the Absolute. In this sense, it is no longer a human vision. It is rather a divine vision.

NOTES

1. The paper is based on two lectures which I delivered at Tehran University, Iran, on May 20 and 24, 1972. I take this occasion to express my deep gratitude to Professor Seyyed Hossein Nasr who provided me with the occasion.

2. From Chapter *Genjô Kôan* of the *Shôbô Genzô*.

3. Hakuun Yasutani, *Shôbô Genzô Sankyú, Genjô Kôan* (Tokyo, 1967), 74.

4. Chapter *San Sui Kyô*.

5. The following exposition is based on what Dôgen says on the nature of time in Chapter *U-ji*.

6. I reproduce his words somewhat freely for a strictly literal translation could not possibly help encumbering the flow of thought with constant explanatory words between parentheses.

7. The expression: "my timeless Now" means the metaphysical Timelessness as I am now actually aware of it in the state of profound contemplation.

8. By *'irfán* or *'irfánic* philosophy I understand in this paper a peculiar form of philosophy that has developed in Islam, a peculiar pattern of philosophizing in which rational thinking is guided by, and goes hand in hand with, spiritual realization through contemplative self-discipline. Also referred to as *hikmat* philosophy.

9. This "domain" includes at its primitive stages the domain of sensation as well.

10. I have already explained the supreme importance of this distinction in Hamadání's thought structure in the two previous chapters of this work: "Mysticism and the Linguistic Problem of Equivocation in the Thought of 'Ayn al-Qudát Hamadání," and "Creation and the Timeless Order of Things: A Study in the Mystical Philosophy of 'Ayn al-Qudát Hamadání."

11. Hamadání, *Náme-há-ye 'Ayn al-Qudát-e Hamadání*, Epistle XIX, ed. 'Afif 'Oseyrán and 'Alínaqí Munzawí, (Tehran 1969), 166.

12. Since I have already fully discussed this part of Hamadání's thought in the previous chapter ("Creation and the Timelessness Order of Things," 120-142), I shall not go further into details here. I would only point out the possibility that Hamadání may have borrowed these two expressions, "God's Face" and God's withness," with their peculiar metaphysical content from Abú Hamid Muhammad al-Ghazálí. In his *Mishkát al-anwár*, ed. A. Afifi (Cairo, 1964), 55-56, Ghazálí, in elucidating the Qur'anic sentence: *kullu sha'in hálikun illá waja-hu* (Surah 28:88), intererprets "God"s Face" exactly in the same way as Hamadání, and in explaining the meaning of the expression allah akbar, he speaks of the "withness" of God with exactly the same metaphysical interpretation.

13. Hamadání, *Zubdat al-haqá'iq*, ed. Afif Osseiran (Teheran, 1962), 60.

14. Ibid.

15. Ibid, 60-61.

16. Muhammad Láhíjí, *Mafátih al-'ijáz fi sharh-e Gulshan-e Ráz*, ed. Kayvan Sami'i (Teheran, 1956), 126-27.

17. Ibn 'Arabí, *Fusús al-hikam*, ed. A. Affifi (Beirut, 1954), 119-26. English translation by R. W. J. Austin, *The Bezels of Wisdom* (New York: The Paulist Press, 1980).

18. On this point, see my *The Concept and Reality of Existence* (Tokyo: Keio Institute of Cultural and Linguistic Studies, 1971), 35-55.

19. Ibn 'Arabí, *Fusús al-hikam*, 122.

20. Hamadání, *Zubdat al-haqá'iq*, 62.

21. Ibn 'Arabi, *Fusús al-hikam*, 125.

CHAPTER 7

EXISTENTIALISM
EAST AND WEST

THE MAIN SUBJECT of this concluding chapter is a comparative consideration of the contemporary existentialism of the West as represented by Martin Heidegger and Jean-Paul Sartre on the one hand, and on the other, the *wahdat al-wujúd* type of philosophy as represented by Mullá Hádí Sabzawárí (d. 1878 C.E.) and his predecessors in Iran.

At first glance one might get the impression that the very formulation of this subject, putting European existentialists like Heidegger and Sartre and Iranian theosophers like Mulla Sadrá and Sabzawárí together into one single arena of comparison, is a bit far-fetched and unnatural. One might reasonably doubt whether it is justifiable at all to treat these thinkers of the East and West together under the title of existentialism on the sole ground that the representatives of the two schools of thought happen to be using one and the same word "existence" as the central key-term of their philosophical systems.

One might go a step further and say that there is hardly any significant relationship to be found between the two. Certainly, the key-term of the *wahdat al-wujúd* philosophy is *wujúd*, an Arabic word which exactly corresponds to the English word *existence* (*Existenz* in German, *existence* in French). But we would commit a grave mistake if, on the basis of this linguistic coincidence alone, we should call the position of the Iranian philosophers "existentialism" and then put it side by side with the existentialism of Heidegger and Sartre, as if they were two variants of one single basic philosophical trend. For it might well be a case of *ishtirák-e lafzí*, i.e. "homonymy," in which one single word is in reality two different words in terms of what they mean. It might he that Western existentialism and Iranian existentialism have very little in common beyond the word. We might well be using the term *existentialism*—and consequently the word *existence* itself—in two different senses, without being aware of the semantic confusion we ourselves might be creating. I shall, in what follows, try to show that such is in reality not the case.

In so doing, however, I must make it clear at the outset that I do not deny the existence of a wide gap separating Western existentialism and Iranian existentialism from one another. The gap is too obvious to remain unnoticed by anybody. The contemporary existentialism of the West is undoubtedly a product of this particular historical epoch of ours which is characteristically dominated by physical science and its human adaptation, i.e. technology. The technological agglomeration of the life-order in highly industrialized modern society in the West has thrown man into an incurable isolation. The life-order created by technology is in reality a disorder in the sense that it is a vast and elaborate system of meaninglessness or absurdity. Man is forced to live in a huge dehumanized mechanism whose meaning he himself does not understand and, which, moreover, constitutes a standing menace to his individuality and personality. In such a situation, modern man necessarily becomes alienated from Nature and from his own self.

Contemporary Western existentialism is a philosophy of the alienated man who is so typically represented by Meursault, the hero of the famous novel of Albert Camus, *Etranger*. It is no wonder that, in such a situation, the kind of "existence" which forms the main concern of the modern existentialist is not existence in general; it is his *own* individual, personal existence, nothing else. Existence here is always *my* existence primarily. Then it is *your* existence, *his* or *her* existence. Existentialism in this sense is a philosophical worldview which takes its start from, and evolves around *this* particular existence which is irreducibly mine, the existence which I myself am doomed to live whether I like it or not.

Thus it comes about that Western existentialism formulates itself through such characteristic key-terms as "uneasiness," "anxiety," "care," "project," "death," "freedom," etc.. And its philosophizing, as is exemplified by the works of the later Heidegger, naturally tends to end up by becoming a lyrical expression of the human pathos in the very midst of non-human, inhuman factual surroundings.

Alongside of this type of philosophy, the existentialism of the Iranian thinkers, clothed in the armor of an intricate system of abstract concepts, might seem at first sight quite colorless, bleak, and chilly. Instead of the note of passion and lyricism which is so characteristic of the German and French existentialists, we see here an abstract and logical thinking being calmly and systematically developed in a rarefied air of reason and intellect, having nothing to do with the mundane problems of daily life. The central problem here is not *my* or *your* personal existence. It is existence in general. It is existence as something supra-personal, universal, and therefore, it might seem, essentially of an abstract nature. Thus we might easily be led to the conclusion that the "existence" which the Western existentialists talk about is completely different from what is meant by the word *wujúd* in the Iranian philosophy of *wahdat al-wujúd.*

However, before we come to any hasty conclusion concerning this problem, we must consider the very important fact that, in spite of all these and still other outward differences between the Western and the Eastern existentialism, the two schools agree with each other on one essential point which concerns the deepest stratum of existential experience itself. In order to notice this point, we have only to apply an elementary phenomenological procedure of *epoché* to what the representative thinkers of these two schools have developed in a theoretical form.

Let us, for this purpose, remove from Western existentialism all the secondary factors, by putting them phenomenologically between parentheses, and try to bring out the structure of the most fundamental vision or experience of "existence." Let us try to break, on the other hand, the seemingly unbreakable shell of conceptualization that covers the entire surface of the metaphysics of a Sabzawárí, and to penetrate into the depth of the mystical or *'irfání* experience itself on which is based the *wahdat al-wujúd* type of philosophizing. Then we shall notice with amazement how close these two kinds of philosophy are to each other in their most basic structure. For it will become evident to us that both go back to one and the same root experience, or primary vision, of the reality of existence. This primary vision is known in Islam as *asálat al-wujúd,* i.e. the "fundamental reality of existence." It constitutes the very core of the whole system of Sabzawárí's metaphysics. Let me first elucidate this concept in plain language, so that we might have an appropriate starting point for the discussion of our problem.

We are living in this world surrounded by an infinite number of things. There are tables and chairs. There are mountains, valleys, stones, and trees. Each one of these things which surround us is, philosophically or ontologically, called *mawjūd,* i.e. "existent," "that-which-is," "that-which-exists," or *das Seiende* in the terminology of Heidegger. Aristotelian metaphysics is precisely a philosophy of "things" understood in this sense. It stands on the assumption that tables, stones, mountains, and trees *are* the ultimately real things. They are real reality, they are the pre-eminently real. This is what is technically known as the Aristotelian concept of "primary substances." And this view of "things" as primary substances accords very well with our common sense. For our common sense, too, naturally tends to consider the concrete individual things that surround us as ultimately real.

The metaphysics of Aristotle has exercised a tremendous influence on the historical formation of ontology, whether Western or Islamic, through medieval scholasticism down to modern times. It is precisely this Aristotelian tradition of ontology that the existentialists of both East and West stand in opposition to. Thus Heidegger in our days reproaches openly and with great emphasis the whole ontological tradition of the West for having been exclusively concerned with "that-which-is," *das Seiende, mawjūd,* totally forgetting the crucial importance to be attached to the small verb *is* which appears in the phrase "that-which-is." What should be the central theme of ontology, he argues, is not "that-which-is" but rather the verb "is," *das Sein,* which forms seemingly quite an insignificant part of this phrase.

Fundamentally of the same nature is the position taken by Jean-Paul Sartre with regard to the true significance of the verb "be." "Existence" is a technical term of philosophy. In ordinary speech we express the same idea by the verb "be." We say for example: "The sky is blue." But this verb *is* is such a tiny word. It is a word with an extremely impoverished semantic content, so impoverished indeed that it has almost no substantial meaning of its own. When we say, "The sky is blue," the verb *is* plays no other role than connecting the predicate (blue) with the subject (sky). Rationally we may know that the verb "to be" means "to exist." But the "existence" we vaguely think of, or imagine behind the word "be" is, as Sartre points out, almost nothing: "My head is empty," as he says.

But in reality, Sartre goes on to assert, behind this seemingly innocent and insignificant verb *is* appearing in "The sky is blue," there is hidden the whole plenitude of existence. But man ordinarily is not at all aware of the fact. This lack of awareness is clearly shown by the very form of the proposition: "The sky is blue," where existence curls itself up, as it were, in the tiniest imaginable form—*is*—and remains in obscurity between the "sky" and "blue." The truth of the matter, according to Sartre, is that in this proposition, or in any other proposition of the same logical or grammatical structure, it is the verb "is," and the verb "is" alone, that points to absolute reality. That is to say, existence alone, nothing else, is the reality. Existence is there, as Sartre says, around us, in us, it is *us*. "I am suffocating: existence penetrates me everywhere, through the eyes, through the nose, through the mouth!" Nevertheless, existence remains hidden. We cannot grasp it by any ordinary means.

It is the awareness of existence in this sense, existence as the ultimate reality, that constitutes the starting point of modern existentialism. The discovery of the significance of what is really meant by the tiny verb "be" has been an event of decisive importance in the history of ontology in the West. Thus, if Heidegger—to come back to him again—so proudly declares that he is accomplishing a revolutionary break with the whole ontological tradition of Western philosophy comparable in importance to the Copernican revolution of Kant, it is due to his conviction that he, of all the Western philosophers, has at last discovered a new key to an authentic ontology by his discovery of the significance of "existence," *das Sein*, as distinguished from "existent," *das Seiende.*

It is interesting to observe, however, that the revolutionary break with the Aristotelian tradition of ontology which Heidegger regards as something unprecedented was already accomplished a long time ago in Islam by the philosophers of the *wahdat al-wujúd* school, whom I shall call here provisionally the Iranian existentialists.

The Iranian existentialists begin by analyzing all concrete things that are found in the world into two basic conceptual components: quiddity and existence. There is nothing in the world that cannot be analyzed into these two components.

Suppose for example there is in our presence a mountain. The "mountain" is different from the "sea." It is different from the "table," "man," or anything else. The "mountain" is different from all other things because it has its own essence which we might call "mountain-ness" and which does not belong to anything other than mountains. This "mountain-ness" is called technically the "quiddity" of mountain. At the same time, this mountain is here, present to us, making itself apparent to our eyes. This actual presence of the mountain here and now is called its "existence." Thus everything in the world is ontologically to be understood as a combination of a quiddity and existence. An actually existing mountain, for example, is a combination of mountain-ness and its actual presence here and now. By the mountain-ness (which is its quiddity), the mountain is differentiated from all other things like chairs, tables, rivers, and valleys. By its "existence" it is here in our presence, making itself apparent to our eyes.

This analysis, however, only and exclusively concerns the *conceptual* structure of things. It only tells us that at the level of conceptual analysis, things are composed of two factors, quiddity and existence. It does not say anything definite about the pre-conceptual structure of reality as it really is in the external world before we begin to analyze it by means of our ready-made concepts.

In brief, the Iranian existentialists take the position that in the pre-conceptual order of things, what is really real is existence, and existence only. Existence is the sole absolute, all-comprehensive Reality that runs through the whole universe. Or rather, the whole universe is nothing other than the reality of existence. All the so-called quiddities are like shadows cast by this absolute Reality as it goes on evolving itself. They are no other than internal modifications or phenomenal forms under which the absolute Reality reveals itself in the empirical dimension of human experience characterized by time-space limitations.

According to this view, we must not understand the proposition "The mountain exists" to mean—as Aristotle certainly would do—that a thing, a primary substance called "mountain," having the quiddity of "mountain-ness," does exist here. The proposition in reality means nothing other than that existence, which is the ultimate Reality and which is the absolute Indeterminate, is here and now manifesting itself in a particular form of self-limitation or self-determination called "mountain." Everything is thus a particular internal modification of the absolute Reality.

Such a view of things, however, obviously goes against our common sense. Unlike Aristotelian metaphysics, which is but a philosophical extension or elaboration of the ordinary common sense view of things, the position taken by the Iranian existentialists lies far beyond the reach of the sober intellect of an ordinary man. The mystery of the absolute ontological truth is disclosed to human consciousness only when it happens to be in an unusually elevated spiritual state, when it is inebriated with the wine of 'irfání experience.

From the earliest periods of the development of philosophy in Iran, metaphysics and mysticism were put into an inseparable relationship with each other. As early as the twelfth century, Suhrawardí (1155-1191 C.E.) gave a definite formulation to the ideal to he consciously pursued by both philosophers and mystics, namely the ideal of an organic unification of spiritual training and the most rigorous conceptual thinking, by declaring that a philosophy that does not culminate in the immediate experience of the absolute Reality is but a vain pastime, while a mystical experience that is not grounded on a rigorous intellectual training is always liable to degenerate into sheer aberration.

Exactly the same attitude was taken toward this problem by another great theosopher of the same period, Ibn 'Arabí (1165-1240 C.E.) who came to the East from Spain. Since then this ideal has established itself as a firmly consolidated tradition in Iran and has produced many outstanding thinkers. Sabzawárí is the ninteenth century representative of this spiritual tradition.

Sabzawárí was in fact an unusually gifted master of mysticism who could at the same time philosophize in a rigorously logical way. The metaphysical system which he developed in his major work (*Sharh-e Manzúmah*) discloses primarily and predominantly this latter aspect of his mind, namely, his logical and rational ability, to such an extent that a careless reader might not even notice that this is a work of a master of mysticism. Yet it is not so difficult to see palpitating just under the surface, the living *'irfání* experience of the reality of existence. In fact, the whole system of his metaphysics is but a philosophical or conceptual elaboration of the original vision of existence, the absolutely absolute Reality as it goes on evolving, modifying itself stage after stage into infinitely variegated phenomenal forms which, as we have seen earlier, are technically known as quiddities.

The position of the *asálat al-wujúd,* the "fundamental reality of existence," of the Iranian existentialists presents a striking similarity to the position taken by modern Western existentialism with regard to the fundamental vision of the reality of existence. Of course, Western existentialism is quite a recent phenomenon, while the Iranian philosophy of *wahdat al-wujúd* has behind itself a centuries-old tradition. It is no wonder that Western existentialism lacks that systematic conceptual perfection which characterizes Iranian philosophy. And yet, precisely because of this crudeness and freshness, it discloses to us nakedly the very nature of the original experience of existence, which remains hidden under the surface of conceptual thinking in the metaphysical system of a Sabzawárí.

Jean-Paul Sartre, for example, has given us a frightfully vivid description of existential experience in his philosophical novel *Nausée.* One day Roquintin, the hero of the novel, finds himself in the park sitting on a bench. A huge chestnut tree is there just in front of him, with its knotty root sunk into the ground under the bench. He is in a state of an extraordinary spiritual tension, a state which is comparable to that which is often experienced in various mystical traditions after a long period of concentrated training. All of a sudden, a vision flashes upon his mind. The ordinary consciousness of concrete, objective individual things disappears. The familiar daily world with all its solidly self-subsistent things crumbles away under his eyes. It is no longer the "root" of a tree that is there in front of him. There is no longer any substance called "chestnut tree." All words disappear; all names that have been scribbled over everywhere by linguistic habits fade away, and together with them the significance of things, their ways of usage, their conceptual associations. Instead, Roquintin sees only soft, monstrous masses, something like dough, in utter disorder, naked in a frightful, obscene nakedness. He is here witnessing existence itself.

It is highly important to notice that in describing his existential experience, i.e. his first encounter with the "dough of all things," he says that "all words disappear." All words disappear, that is to say, all names that have hitherto marked off all things one from the other as so many independent substances, suddenly fall off and vanish from his consciousness. In the particular terminology of Iranian philosophy, this event may aptly be described by saying that the quiddities lose before his own eyes their seeming solidity or reality and begin to disclose their *i'tibárí* nature, i.e. their original ficticiousness. The quiddities, the "chestnut-ness," "tree-ness," "root-ness," etc., consolidated by these linguistic forms, have in the past formed, so to speak, an insulating screen between him and the immediate vision of the all-pervading existence. It is only when these obstacles are removed that the reality of existence appears naked to man's eyes. It is upon such an unusual vision of the "dough" of things that existentialism, whether of the East or the West, is based.

I have tried in the foregoing to bring to light the most fundamental ontological intuition that seems to underlie both the contemporary existentialism of the West and the *wahdat al-wujúd* type of Iranian philosophy. It is indeed interesting to note that an identical ontological intuition constitutes the very basis and the starting-point of all philosophizing for these two forms of existentialism.

It is no less interesting to observe that, starting from the basically identical vision of existence the philosophers of the two schools, one in the East and the other in the West, have produced two types of philosophy that are almost completely different from each other. But no wonder. As I have noted at the outset, the existentialism of the West is a child of this particular age of ours, in which the exorbitant development of technology has produced, and is actually producing, the most drastic convulsions in human life; an age in which human life itself is in imminent danger of being strangled and stifled by the very products of the human brain. Besides, most of the leading existentialists are professedly atheists.

The *wahdat al-wujúd* philosophy, on the contrary, owes its birth and formation to completely different historical circumstances. It is a product of past ages, a product of a long spiritual tradition, supported by a markedly religious background. This, of course, should not be taken to mean that the Iranian existentialists have always lived in a serene atmosphere of spirituality. A long list of martyrs alone attests eloquently to the fact that they, too, had to pass through the most formidable crises, that they had to face desperate difficulties besetting their times. But their existential—in the contemporary Western acceptation of the word—trepidations did not affect in any essential way the products of their philosophizing. Philosophy in those ages was not yet so vitally involved in the mundane problems of daily life. For, in philosophizing, the eyes of the philosophers were definitely directed toward the eternal order of things.

It is obvious that each of the two types of existentialism has its own peculiar strengths and weaknesses from the viewpoint of the function to be performed by philosophy in the present-day intellectual situation of the world. The existentialism of the West will have much to learn from its Oriental counterpart by way of overcoming the cultural nihilism toward which the West seems to be irresistibly drawn under the crushing power of the mechanization of life.

But Oriental philosophy, on its part, does not seem to be able to maintain its spiritual values in the face of the pressing problems that naturally arise from the actualities of our days. If it is to remain just as it has been in the past, it will find itself utterly powerless in the presence of our manifold contemporary problems. For technology is no longer a Western phenomenon and is rapidly extending its sway over the whole globe. And this actual situation is creating countless historical problems that humanity has never faced before in history. The philosophy of a Sabzawārī, if left untouched in its medieval form would seem to be no longer in a position to cope with these new problems.

It is my conviction that the time has come when we must begin making efforts to revive the creative energy contained in this kind of philosophy in such a way that its spirit might be resuscitated in the form of a new philosophic worldview powerful enough and alive enough to cope with the new problems peculiar to the new historical epoch into which we have just entered. Such, it would seem, is the intellectual task that is imposed upon us. And in the course of carrying out this task, we Orientals shall and must learn precious lessons from the way contemporary Western existentialism is struggling to solve the problems of human existence in the very midst of the dehumanizing and dehumanized structure of modem society. I believe, only through this kind of intellectual collaboration will the much hoped for philosophical convergence of East and West be actualized.

INDEX OF NAMES & TECHNICAL TERMS

'adam (non-existent) 26, 46, 52,
    159; *'adam-e aslí* (original
    nothingness) 59; *'adamíyat-e aslí*
    (fundamental nothingness) 46
adhyása (superimposition)) 28, 74
ahadíyah (absolute oneness) 57, 59,
    64, 87-89, 91, 93, 97-98
'álam-e saghír (man as microcosm)
    62
Ámulí, Haydar 8, 9, 25-26, 31-32,
    82, 84
aná'l-haqq (I am the Absolute) 54,
    98, 107
Aquinas, Thomas 3, 4
Archetypes (see *a'yán al-thábitah*)
'ard (breadth, horizontal order) 113
'árif (gnostic) 122, 161-62
Aristotle 39-40, 178, 181
Ash'arites 168-69
asmá' wa-sifát (divine names and
    attributes) 28, 92
Átman 77
Augustine, Saint 127
Averroes (see Ibn Rushd)
Avicenna (see Ibn Síná)
avidyá (ignorance) 28, 79, 90
'awámm (common people) 21
a'yán al-thábitah (eternal arche-
    types) 52 , 92-93
'ayn al-basírah (eye of spiritual
    vision) 41
'ayn al-marífah (eye of gnostic
    cognition) 100

baqá' (survival) 14-20, 25, 42-43,
    54-57, 59, 77, 79, 133
barzakh (intermediary stage) 62
Bastámí, Báyazíd 107-08, 120, 162
bátil (unreal) 20, 59
bátin (esoteric, concealed) 13, 85-
    86, 92, 142
bi-shart lá (existence as negatively
    conditioned) 88, 96

bi-shart shay' (existence as
    conditioned by being-some-
    thing) 96
Brahman 10, 28, 33, 73-74, 77, 80-
    81; *Brahma-pratya-yasantair
    jagat* (world is a continuous
    series of cognitions of Brahman)
    10; *dvi-rúpa Brahma* (two-fold
    Brahman) 86; *nirguna Brahman*
    (unconditioned, attributeless
    Brahman) 28, 86; *sirguna
    Brahman* (Brahman with
    attributes) 86; *parabrahman*
    (Supreme Brahman) 34
bu'd (distance, remoteness) 105-07
Buddhism 19, 29, 60, 69, 76, 86, 91

Camus, Albert 176
chén ju (truly such, the absolute) 76
Chu Tzu 36
Chuang Tzu 17, 37, 78, 88
coincidentia oppositorium 19, 25,
    34, 45
Confucianism 33, 36, 69, 86

darkness (see *zulmah*)
das Seiende (existent, *mawjúd*) 178,
    180
datsu raku shin jin (dropped-off-
    mind-and-body) 14
dhat al-wujúd (existence itself,
    absolute existence) 86-87, 96-97
dhawq (tasting of spiritual
    experience) 11
dhawu al-'aql (people of reason,
    philosphers) 21; *dhawu al-'aql
    wa-al-'ayn* (people of reason and
    intuition) 21; *dhawu al-'ayn*
    (people of intuition, mys-
    tics) 21; *dhu al-'aynayn* (man of
    two eyes) 19, 84
díde-ye bátin (inner eye) 57
Dógen 36-37, 142-50, 155

Existence (see *wujúd*)
Existentialism 75-76, 174-86

faná' (annihilation) 11-20, 25, 37,
    42-43, 53, 55, 57, 59, 77, 79, 133;
    faná' ba'da al-baqá (annihilation
    after survival) 60; *faná'-ye faná'*
    (annihilation of annihilation) 12
al-Fárábí 4, 70
farq (separation) 16, 54; *farq ba'd
    al-jam'* (separation after
    unification) 16
fayd (effusion) 13; *fayd aqdas* (most
    sacred emanation) 89; *fayd
    muqaddas* (sacred emana-
    tion) 93
al-Ghazálí, Abú Hámid 99, 102
al-Ghazálí, Ahmad 99, 119
gháyat al-tashábuh (extremity of
    equivocation) 104
ghayb (mystery) 87; *ghayb al-
    ghuyúb* (Mystery of Myster-
    ies) 88
ghayr (other) 47, 55, 96
God: God's Face (see *wajh alláh*);
    dhat alláh (the Essence of
    God) 86; God's knowl-
    edge 108-16, 132-34; God's
    withness (see *ma'íyah*); as a
    hidden treasure 91; *kamálát
    dhátíyah* (essential perfections of
    God) 92
Greek philosophy 4, 70

habs kardan (chaining) 160
al-Halláj, Mansur 54, 98, 107-08,
    120
Hamadání, 'Ayn al-Qudát 98-117,
    119-39, 150-58, 167
haqq (Absolute Reality) 59, 64, 81;
    haqíqah núráníyah (luminous
    reality) 45
hastí (existence) 64; *hastí-ye mutlaq*
    (absolute existence) 45, 52, 57
Heidegger, Martin 174, 176, 178,
    180, 182

Henle, Paul 40
hijáb (veil) 38, 49
hikmat philosophy 99, 120, 142,
    159
hsüan chih yu hsüan (Mystery of
    Mysteries) 37, 88
hubb (love) 91
hudúr (presence) 11
hun tun (chaos) 17
huwíyah (he-ness) 165

Ibn 'Arabí 2, 26, 66, 93, 99, 119-
    20, 151, 160-73, 184
Ibn Rushd 3-4, 70
Ibn Síná 3–5, 70, 113-14
idáfah (relation) 80; *idáfah
    ishráqíyah* (illuminative
    relation) 80, 118
'ilm (knowledge) 108-9, 114
imkán dhátí (ontological
    possibility) 159
infitáh 'ayn al-basírah (opening the
    eye of spiritual vision) 100
'irfán (gnosis) 151, 153, 177, 182-83
ishráq (illumination) 11, 41
Ismailism 25
i'tibárí (fictitiousness) 44, 58, 83
ittihád al-'álim wa-al-ma'lúm
    (unification of the knower and
    the known) 7

jam' (gathering) 16, 55; *jam' al-
    jam'* 16, 18
Jámí, 'Abd al-Rahmán 12, 22, 162
jan fa (things of defilment) 74
ji-ji-muge-hokka (ontological
    dimension of unobstructed
    mutual interpenetration of all
    things) 60
Jílí, 'Abd al-Karím 81-82, 87

Kai, Zen Master 146
kashf (unveiling) 13, 76
khalq (creature, creation) 58, 81;
    khalq jadíd (perpetual creation)
    138, 141-71

khawáss (privileged people,
mystics) 21; khawáss al-khawáss
(privileged of all privileged,
gnostics) 21

lá bi-shart maqsamí (existence as
absolutely non-conditioned) 94,
96
lá-shay (non-thing) 46, 115
Láhíjí, Muhammad Gilání 9, 19, 29,
38-63, 159-60
Lao Tzu 27, 88-89

ma'dúm (non-existent) 116, 133,
157
Mahayana Buddhism 12, 74, 82, 90
máhíyah (quiddity) 4, 28-29, 52,
71, 75, 180-81
ma'íyat alláh (God's withness) 112-
15, 135, 154
malakút (spiritual world) 103
mashí'ah (will) 128
mawjúd (existent) 70, 75, 116, 133,
157, 178
máyá (self-conditioning power
inherent in Brahman) 28, 90
mazáhir (manifest) 84
Moses 8
muhál al-wujúd (impossible to
exist) 127; muhál bi-dháti-hi
(impossible by itself) 129;
muhál bi-ghayri-hi (impossible
by something else) 129
mulk (phenomenal world) 103
mumkin (possible) 20, 58, 64, 126,
159; mumkin bi-dháti-hi
(possible by itself) 129
muqábalah (turning toward
God) 115
Mystery of Mysteries 91, 93, 95

nafas rahmání (breath of Mercifulness) 94, 160
náma-rúpa (name-and-form) 28,
78
nikon (timeless now) 148

nirvana 77
nisbah (relation) 115, 131, 156
nístí-ye mutlaq (absolute nothingness) 57
núr (light) 9, 38, 44, 100, 108; núr
al-wujúd (the light of existence)
132, 157; núr al-wujúd al-azalí
(the light of Eternal existence)
130; núr fí al-bátin (inner
light) 122, 152; núr-e mutlaq
(absolute light) 45; núr-e siyáh
(black light) 55, 57; núr-e
wujúd (light of existence) 48
Núrbakhshíyah 39

parameshvara (Supreme Lord) 33
Perfect Man 81, 162, 166, 171

qadím (pre-eternal) 124
qalb (heart) 161; qalb al-'árif (heart
of the mystic) 163-64
Qaysarí, Dá'úd 87
qudra (divine power) 127
quiddity (see máhíyah)
qurb (nearness) 105-7

rahmah (Mercy) 94; rahmah
wujúdíyah (existential mercy of
God) 28
rutba (ontological rank) 132

Sabzawárí, Mullá Hádí 174, 177,
182
Sadrá, Mullá (Sadra al-Dín
Muhammad Shírází) 2, 7-8,
66, 78, 158
Sartre, Jean-Paul 174, 178, 183-84
Sat (pure being, existence) 73
sawád-e a'zam (supreme blackness) 57
Shabastarí, Mahmúd 9, 20, 29,
38-63
Shankara 10, 74, 78, 80-82
shin jin datsu raku (mind-and-
body-dropping off) 13
shuhúd (inner witnessing) 11

shúnyatá (nothingness) 12
siyáhí (blackness) 56; *siyah-rú'í* (black-facedness) 46
subhání (glory be to me!) 107
Suhrawardí, Shiháb al-Dín Yahyá 41, 44, 64, 99, 119-20, 182
svabháva (self-nature) 29

tabaddul al-'álam ma'a al-anfás (transformed with each breath) 166
t'ai chi (Supreme Ultimate) 34, 36, 87
tajallí (divine self-manifestation) 20, 28-29, 48, 58, 62, 92, 163-64
takhlís (cleansing the mind) 12
tao (the way) 27, 89, 91
Taoism 17, 27, 69, 74, 78, 86
taqallub (the constant change or transformation of the heart) 164-65
taqyid (determination) 26
táríkí-ye kathrat (darkness of multiplicity) 49
tashábuh (equivocation) 101-07, 123
tashakhkhus (individuation) 58
tathatá (suchness, the absolute) 76; *tathágata-garbha* (Storehouse of the Absolute) 91
tawhíd (unification) 12; *tawhíd wujúdí* (unification of existence) 26
tawr al-'aql (domain of reason) 121, 151; *tawr wará'a al-'aql* (the domain beyond reason) 100, 121, 151
té (virtues) 27
Temple of Light 62
Time 93, 136-38, 156; imaginary time 154; timelessness 136–138, 148, 172; timeless now 149

Un Mon, Zen Master 147

Vedanta 10, 24-25, 34, 73-75, 77-78, 86, 90
vyávahárika-reality (relative reality) 81

wahdat al-wujúd 26, 29, 34, 44, 47, 52, 60, 66-97, 120, 175, 177,
wáhidíyah (oneness) 65, 89, 93, 96-97
wahj alláh (God's Face) 115, 124, 131-33, 154; *wajh-e hastí* (face of existence) 50; *wajh-e nístí* (face of non-existence) 49
Wittgenstein, Ludwig 23, 101
wu (non-existence) 37; *wu chi* (Ultimate Nothingness) 34, 86; *wu wu* (non-non-existence) 37; *wu-wu-wu* (non-non-non-Being) 88
wujúd (existence) 3–4, 26, 29, 34, 44, 64, 70, 75, 175; *asálat al-wujúd* (fundamental reality of existence) 183; *wujúd bi shart shay'* (existence-as-conditioned-by-being-something) 92; *wujúd i'tibárí* (fictitious existence) 80; *wujúd lá bi-shart qismí* (existence as non-conditioned) 94; *wujúd majází* (metaphorical existence) 80; *yanbú'-e wujúd* (fountainhead of existence) 153

Yasutani, Hakuun 145

záhir (exoteric, manifest) 13, 85, 92, 141
Zen Buddhism 13-14, 36-37, 142-50
zill (shadow) 9, 48
zuhúr núr fí al-bátin (appearance of light in the interior) 100
zulmah (darkness) 38, 45